WATERSHED

Reflections on Water

Grant MacEwan

WITH AN INTRODUCTION BY HUGH DEMPSEY

Afterword by Michael Stock

NEWEST PRESS

Grant
MacEwan
College

Canadian Cataloguing in Publication Data

MacEwan, Grant, 1902-2000
  Watershed

ISBN 1-896300-35-9

I. Watersheds. 2. Water-supply. I. Title.
GB561.M32 2000   553.7   C00-910689-8

Edited by: Christopher Wiebe
Editor for the press: Don Kerr
Cover and interior design: Ruth Linka
Background cover image: D. Shawn Kabatoff / Vision Images

THE CANADA COUNCIL   LE CONSEIL DES ARTS
FOR THE ARTS   DU CANADA
SINCE 1957   DEPUIS 1957

Canadian   Patrimoine
Heritage   canadien

NeWest Press wishes to thank the Grant MacEwan College for their support of, and involvement in this project. NeWest also acknowledges the support of the Canada Council for the Arts and the Alberta Foundation for the Arts for our publishing program. We also acknowledge the financial support of the Government of Canada through the Book Publishing Industry Development Program (BPIDP) for our publishing activities.

The MacEwan family would like to thank NeWest Press, and to extend a special thank you to Dorothy Gray, without whose faith, perseverance, and boundless enthusiasm this book would never have seen the light of day.

Every reasonable effort has been made to acquire permission for copyright material used in this book, and to acknowledge such indebtedness accurately. Any errors and omissions called to the attention of the publisher will be corrected in future editions.

Lorna Crozier's "Rain" has been reprinted by permission of the author. The excerpt from the *Regina Leader Post*, October 18, 1947 has been reprinted by permission. The excerpt from *Survival of a Vision* by George Spence has been reprinted by permission of Agriculture and Agri-Food Canada. The excerpt from *Who Speaks for the Earth* by Barbara Ward has been reprinted by permission of W.W. Norton.

NeWest Press
201-8540-109th Street
Edmonton, Alberta T6G 1E6
(780) 432-9427
www.newestpress.com

00 01 02 03 04   4 3 2 1

PRINTED AND BOUND IN CANADA

To dear old Al Ewen, with whom I was a working partner in the production of several agricultural textbooks and a partner in adventure when we took a poor man's holiday on a log raft on the South Saskatchewan River, and judged it to be the best water adventure of our lives.

So many write of rain
its small hands,
the memories it brings,
the sounds of things it touches.

How it changes what we see,
gives taste to what we thought
was tasteless
　　　　　　　—Lorna Crozier, "Rain"

TABLE OF CONTENTS

ILLUSTRATIONS

Photographs

Maps

INTRODUCTION

This is Grant MacEwan's last book. Sadly, he did not live to see it in print, for he died at the age of ninety-seven on June 15, 2000, just weeks after this manuscript was delivered to the publishers. It was his forty-eighth book and completed a run that started with his first volume, *The Science and Practice of Canadian Animal Husbandry*, published in 1936. That first book was co-authored with A.H. Ewen, the man to whom Grant MacEwan has dedicated this final volume.

For those not already familiar with this western legend, Grant MacEwan was lieutenant governor of Alberta, mayor of Calgary, leader of the provincial Liberal Party, university professor, author, lecturer, and raconteur. Any one of these could have been a lifetime career for anyone else, but Grant MacEwan did them all. He was a vital part of the fabric that made up Alberta and western Canada for the past half century.

Grant was born in Brandon, Manitoba, on August 12, 1902, and grew up on a farm near Melfort, Saskatchewan. As he reached manhood, he pursued his two first loves of agriculture and teaching by receiving degrees from Ontario College of Agriculture, in Guelph, and from Iowa State College. He then served as Professor of Animal Husbandry at the University of Saskatchewan, and later as Dean of Agriculture at the University of Manitoba. He moved to Calgary in 1951 and went on to play an active part in Alberta's political, business, and academic life for the rest of his career. He served as a Calgary alderman for four terms and was mayor of the city from 1963 to 1966. Provincially, he was a Member of the Legislative Assembly from 1955 to 1958 and leader of the provincial Liberal Party. He later went on to become one of the most popular lieutenant governors in the history of Alberta, serving from 1966 to 1974. He put his own stamp on the office, impressing people with his friendliness and his seemingly boundless energy. He outwalked Premier Peter Lougheed in a walk for charity, disdained the use of the official limousine except when necessary, and was probably seen by more people during his term than any other lieutenant governor as he kept up a gruelling schedule of official functions, school visits, and public ceremonies. At these gatherings he usually spoke, often with humour and usually with an inspiring message for the young. After leaving the vice-regal office, he devoted the rest of his life to writing and public speaking.

This tall, gangly man was an impressive figure and greatly admired for his friendliness, his wit, and his razor sharp mind. I considered him to be one of the finest men I ever met and one whom I truly admired. When I first met him in 1957 he was writing columns for the *Calgary Herald*, *The Western Producer* in Saskatoon, and the *Canadian Cattleman* magazine.

After a few discussions, I realized that his knowledge went far beyond agriculture and that he had a lively interest in the history of western Canada.

For the first several years of his career, Grant had been content to write books dealing exclusively with agricultural science. Then in 1942, the Canadian Broadcasting Corporation suggested that he do a series of four broadcasts about western personalities for a program called "Sodbusters." This was his first experience in writing about people, and the program was so well received that he produced several more broadcasts; in 1948 the results were published under the same title as that of the radio program. Now that Grant had "discovered" the pioneers of the West, there was no stopping him. In 1952 he published *Between the Red and the Rockies* which offered a broad history of the prairie provinces. According to his biographer, Rusty Macdonald, this book "could be taken as the master plan for his work extending over the next thirty or forty years... With broad sweeping strokes, he sketched the story of the development of the region that was to become his literary territory and his major interest, in particular agriculture and the people who developed half a continent of nearly empty grassland into a bread basket for the world within one generation." (R.H. Macdonald, *The Best of Grant MacEwan*. Saskatoon: Prairie Books, 1982, xi.)

This interest was evident in 1958 when he published *Fifty Mighty Men*, biographies and stories about early western Canadians such as Father Lacombe, Henry Wise Wood, and Sir Frederick Haultain. These stories had previously appeared as columns in *The Western Producer*. He followed in the next year with the excellent volume, *Calgary Cavalcade*, and over the next decade he published such books as *John Ware's Cow Country, Blazing the Old Cattle Trail, Hoofprints and Hitchingposts*, and *Poking into Politics*. Many of his books featured biographies, such as *And Mighty Women Too* (a sequel to *Fifty Mighty Men*), *Portraits from the Plains* (dealing with prominent native people), and *Métis Makers of History*. Individual volumes concentrated on western figures such as Bob Edwards, John Ware, Jack Morton, Sir Frederick Haultain, and Pat Burns. Grant summed up his philosophy to his son-in-law, Max Foran, when he stated, "I believe that biography is the best way to inspire young people... if you are looking for a good subject for writing and had history in mind, you would have to find somebody who achieved something, wasn't all saint and wasn't all sinner." (Max Foran, ed., *Grant MacEwan's Journals*. Edmonton: Lone Pine Publishing, 1983, 149; George Melnyk, *The Literary History of Alberta*, vol.2. Edmonton: University of Alberta Press, 1999, 108.)

Grant MacEwan was always interested in the environment and he once told a reporter in all seriousness that he promised God he would look after Alberta's soil, trees, creatures, and oil. As part of his personal creed he wrote, "I believe the biggest challenge is in being a helper rather than a destroyer of the treasures in nature's storehouse, a conserver, a husbandman, and partner in caring for the Vineyard." (Cited in *Calgary Herald*, June 17, 2000.) This philosophy was reflected in his writings as early as 1958 when he outlined the efforts of George Spence to conserve the West's water resources and to develop irrigation through the Prairie Farm Rehabilitation

Act. Grant refers to Spence as "an Apostle of Conservation" and offers a quote which is equally appropriate for this present book on water. Spence stated, "It's a crime to allow water to run across this dry land, down to the sea, without making an effort to conserve and use it to augment the scanty supplies natures has given us." (Grant MacEwan, *Fifty Mighty Men*. Saskatoon: Modern Press, 1958, 241)

Grant's first book dealing specifically with the environment was *Entrusted to My Care*, produced in 1966, long before the subject had become popular. According to Macdonald, in this book "Grant MacEwan dealt with the principle that had guided him all his life—the principle of conservation" (Macdonald, 1982, xvi). In it, he makes a strong argument for the fact that Man has a responsibility to protect the environment rather than trying to destroy it through aggressive exploitation. His current—and final—book continues this theme by examining the role of water in our history and environment.

Over the years, Grant's books, public speaking, and political career meant that he was usually in the news and was the subject of praise and admiration for his dedication to the people and the environment of western Canada. He was also well known as a man who believed in the principles of thrift, honesty, and helping his fellow man. In the city, he often took a transit bus to work and while travelling to other cities, the Greyhound bus was his main means of travel. He became so well known for this practise that on his eighty-eighth birthday, Greyhound Lines of Canada gave him a lifetime pass and made him on honorary bus driver. On another occasion, the Calgary Fire Department asked him how much he would charge to write a history of their organization. A jar of peanut butter was his response. He wrote their history, *100 Years of Smoke, Sweat and Tears*, with the proceeds going to the Calgary Fire Fighters Burn Treatment Fund.

In recognition of his great service to his country, Grant was awarded the Order of Canada, five honorary university doctorates, the Haultain Prize for excellence, and just a month before his death, he was on hand to receive the Golden Pen Lifetime Achievement Award from the Alberta Writers Guild. That was his last public appearance. In addition, Grant MacEwan College in Edmonton is named after him, as is MacEwan Hall at the University of Calgary, and Grant MacEwan Elementary School in Calgary. He and his family also established the MacEwan Family Charitable Fund, the Grant MacEwan Nature Protection Fund, and the Grant MacEwan Community Fund, all of which are administered by the Calgary Foundation.

At the time of his passing, messages of condolence came from far and near. The Alberta government announced the launching of a literary award and a United World College Scholarship fund in his name while a letter-to-the-editor suggested that the Spray Valley Provincial Park near Canmore be renamed in his honour. A common expression by many Albertans at the time of his death was that they had never met him but they felt as if they knew him, either through his books or because they had heard him speak. To them, he was a man who inspired confidence in the positive aspects of life and of the old values of hard work, thrift, and honesty. Someone recalled that each time he spoke while he was lieutenant governor, he planted a white elm tree as a message of hope for the future.

Because of the love Albertans had for him, Grant MacEwan was accorded a state funeral—the first in the province in almost forty years. He lay in state in the Legislative Building in Edmonton and impressive ceremonies were held both in the capital and in Calgary. In paying tribute to him, the current lieutenant governor, Lois Hole, stated, "His remarkable life will serve as an inspiration for future generations of Albertans" (*Calgary Herald*, June 17, 2000).

Grant MacEwan worked on this current book during the last two or three years of his life. It is a potpourri of facts, reminiscences, and comments. The central theme, of course, is water, and with this in mind he has ranged over much of the world and over vast eons of time to tell his story. This book is not so much a single tale about water, but a summary of Grant's lifetime of observations. There are the western Canadian themes of irrigation, water conservation, and the disasters caused by the flooding Red River. He tells of schemes to haul icebergs to California for fresh water, and of diverting Canadian streams to the United States. He writes about many people whose careers were closely allied with water. He revisits the life of George Spence, then tells a wonderful story of a raft trip he made on the South Saskatchewan River with his old friend Al Ewen.

This book, then, is a fitting conclusion to the career of Grant MacEwan. Just as he was far-reaching in his interests, so is this book far-reaching in its subject matter. Just as Grant was passionately interested in the environment, so does this book emphasize the importance of water to the world. And just as he was interested in people, so does this book look at the accomplishments of individuals.

Grant, we'll miss you.

Hugh A. Dempsey
Chief Curator Emeritus
Glenbow Museum, Calgary.

PART I: GROUNDWATER

The world's water appears to be in a constant state of uneasy movement. It moves in great haste like the Slave River rapids of northern Alberta, and at the incomprehensibly slow pace of groundwater seeping through silt or sand deep underground in southern Saskatchewan. Sooner or later it will reach a junction in the water cycle and start all over again, undiminished and unchanging, the perfect symbol of timelessness.

Any settlers of the Canadian West who discovered a groundwater spring on their new homesteads knew that they were very lucky. Celebrations of thanksgiving were in order, especially when the water was of good quality. For these new settlers flocking to the prairies, the salt water of the oceanic variety was not one of their worries, but rather the much-despised alkali water. Alkali water (high in concentrated sodium or magnesium) has laxative qualities, and is one reason why newcomers to the prairies, who had no choice but to drink this water, had difficulty in obtaining a good night's

Alberta's first power water wheel, built by John Swift near Jasper. The quest for healthy water and the means to transport it were primary concerns for settlers in Saskatchewan and Alberta.
(Provincial Archives of Alberta, A-3008)

sleep. Cattle and horses, having no other choice of beverage, drank the alkali water and probably suffered more than they were able to express.

For the farmer who was unhappy with the paucity of water in his well, or its high concentration of alkali, the only hope for immediate relief was hauling household drinking water from the well of a neighbour who had happened to be lucky in his strike. It was an arrangement that was quite satisfactory for a short time, but the necessity of hitching a team to a stoneboat, sleigh or wagon and driving several miles with a barrel of water was bound to become tiresome. Invariably the farmer's decision was to call a government well-drilling team to return for another attempt to find the ever elusive groundwater.

My parents—Alex, a stubborn Scot, and Bertha, a pious Presbyterian—were among the many Western Canadian pioneers of the homesteading period whose disappointing experiences tested their spirits but never broke their will to try one more time. The year 1915 found the MacEwan family fallen on hard times on a piece of unbroken land in central Saskatchewan. The land was of the finest quality and they were fortunate to own it, though they could lay claim to very little else of value. They had no house or shelter, no stable, no livestock aside from the two ancient horses that their previous owner seemed glad to sell for a thrifty twenty-five dollars each. They owned no cattle, except the Jersey cow that had supplied milk for the family in Brandon, no fence, not even a single acre under cultivation, no farm machinery, unless the push-mower used on the lawn in the city counted, no cultivated ground big enough for a garden and no cash income. The only poultry consisted of twelve hens that belonged to their thirteen-year-old son, Grant, in what had started as a city backyard project housed in two piano boxes. The biggest hardship of all was the scarcity of water. They didn't have a well and their water had to be hauled in from a neighbour's. But they did have a post-hole digger and a determination to tap into the groundwater that must, they were sure, run beneath their land.

The story of how the MacEwan family found themselves in this predicament was a sad one which many settlers experienced in the boom period of 1905 to 1913. Father MacEwan had come West in 1889 and had farmed successfully at Brandon until yielding to the temptation to sell the perfectly good half-section farm in 1908 and relocate to the city of Brandon. The economy in "The Wheat City" was booming and speculation and profits were in the air. MacEwan joined in and invested heavily in the city property market which promised to soar in value and make him a quick fortune.

But city life did not last long. MacEwan went bankrupt when real estate values plunged with the commencement of the First World War and he could no longer service his debts. In a moment of frustration he unloaded a few parcels of city real estate, sight unseen, in exchange for a farm of five quarters at Margo, Saskatchewan, which was said to be mostly cultivated and ready for cropping, with a barnyard stocked with cattle, farm machinery and work horses. Presumably the attractive Margo farm had everything, even a lake with sandy beaches and hungry fish. In short order, MacEwan was loading a train car with settlers' effects that included the family furniture, two old horses for which he could raise the fifty dollars for purchase, the family milk cow and the lawnmower—an item that may have helped to qualify the load of freight as settlers' belongings. Since MacEwan was out of money by this time and could only purchase one train ticket, Grant was forced to ride along as a stowaway. The two departed on April 17, 1915 with the understanding that Mrs. MacEwan and George, then nine years old, would come later when the home on the Margo farm had been made ready.

As fate would have it, the home on the new farm was never to be made ready. First of all, the new owners could not find it. They couldn't find the eight horses, the harnesses or the farm machinery either. In fact, they didn't exist. The land trade was a classic case of misrepresented goods.

If MacEwan's problems seemed serious before, they were now doubly compounded. Fortunately, in the course of a conference between the father and his thirteen-year-old son, the former recalled to his own surprise that he thought he still owned a section of land near Melfort, Saskatchewan. He had bought the land on speculation about a decade before and promptly forgot about it. "We'll reload our freight," the father decided, "and re-bill to Melfort. We'll set our minds to turning that piece of land into a first-rate farm." Grant was ready for anything, and the train car was duly re-directed to Prince Albert to be switched to the Melfort line. The ill-fated Margo farm was left to the care of the family lawyer in Brandon.

A telegram was sent to Mrs. MacEwan in Brandon telling her not to come out until better arrangements had been made. Father and son arrived at Melfort where they found, by merciful good luck, that the farm had escaped both sale and mortgage. The first full day at Melfort was a Sunday. Father and son decided to take some bread and cheese and walk to the land which the elder MacEwan had not seen for a decade. It was seven kilometres to the land, overgrown with willow and poplar bluffs, but covered with lush peavine fodder. When they sank their spade into the sod and turned it over, however, it was plain, even to the untrained eye, that the black loam beneath them was of the highest possible grade.

1915 was a spectacular year in Western Canada. For those who had cropland ready for planting, it was a year when Nature's best efforts came together for near-ideal growing conditions. It produced a bumper crop of which pioneers had never seen the like and of which they never ceased to boast. The bankrupt MacEwans were present to see it happen but, having no broken land to seed, were unable to benefit from this burst of Nature's extravagance.

Unwilling repatriates to the land, the new residents on Section 23, Township 44, Range 19 West of the 2nd Meridian were people who had known a moderately high standard of living, but had been rudely reduced to the humblest conditions. Some complaining might have been expected, but Mrs. MacEwan—mother, nurse, and angel in disguise in a new rural community still short of medical services—resolved that it was not going to happen. George and Grant registered at Spry School, a three-kilometre walk from the farm, and had daily chores before and after school, all of which eased the threat of boredom or despondency. Everybody had his or her job to do and everybody found the shack bedroom a blessing at the end of the day.

One by one, the pioneer tasks began to shrink. The family cut 1,600 willow fence pickets for fencing. While they were still using a neighbour's granary for bedrooms, MacEwan heard about a one-room shack with a shanty roof that cost twenty-five dollars and could be placed on a wagon and hauled to the farm. He said he had been saving money for just such a purpose and closed the deal on the shack. The next day the house—flattered by the term—arrived at its new location, and was soon resting on four big stones. The family's two iron beds were set up and everyone slept under the family's own roof for a change. The shack was not beautiful but soon the unpainted structure, five by five-and-a-half metres, displayed signs of homey comfort. Using his land as collateral, MacEwan obtained a bank loan and engaged Jack Curtis, a farmer who owned a twenty-five horsepower, one-cylinder gasoline tractor, to come with his four-bottom plow and break fifty acres for cropland to be farmed in 1916.

A third horse was bought, a lightweight called Bill, who was strong enough to supplement the power of the other two ageing but heavier horses. With borrowed equipment, much of the remaining season was given to cultivating the newly broken ground. Throughout days and evenings for the rest of the year, a stable was constructed from lumber and green poplar poles for framing scantlings. Though he was encouraged by this progress, MacEwan knew he now had no choice but to make the search for water his leading enterprise. Nothing was more important than overcoming the wasted energy and expense of hauling water for the livestock and household from a neighbour's well.

MacEwan enquired about the provincially-owned well-boring machine. He found that, while the machine had been highly regarded, it had been withdrawn from public use. There was a privately-owned machine ready for custom boring, but it was expensive to hire and its operator required immediate payment. By coincidence, one of the metal items in the boxcar load of settlers' effects from Brandon was a posthole auger eighteen centimetres in diameter with a metre-long metal pipe stem detachable by the removal of two nuts and bolts. MacEwan took it out, straightened its metal blades and saw that it produced a fairly clean round hole. He then asked himself if he could not bore a well or test hole with it at almost no cost. The next day he was seen catching a ride to town in a neighbour's democrat, carrying the metal pipe part and the handle of the auger.

Late the next day, he arrived home reporting another buggy ride during which he had had the good fortune to visit the town scrap pile. He had recovered an armful of discarded one-inch pipe, and had persuaded the local plumber to cut the pipe in one metre lengths and drill two holes in each piece for connections. He returned to the scrap pile to see what luck he might have in finding some odds and ends that resembled metal couplings.

He reported to his family that he had had a very successful day, and had spent only one dollar and seventy-five cents. Even that cost had been offset somewhat by the excellent patch of mushrooms he had found beside the scrap pile. Now Alex MacEwan could hardly wait to put his eighteen-centimetre well auger to the test. The biggest challenge was to make the auger's new pipe couplings work. But he was sure that if he could arrange another day at the scrap pile he could improve upon the suitability of the improvised pieces.

One of the nice features about the new well auger was that all four members of the family could take turns operating it when they were not busy with other work. However, problems arose. It was easy to ensure straight vertical penetration in the early stages of the digging, but at a depth of three metres, a loose connection at the joint made for poor directional control. Another problem was the resistance from small stones embedded in the clay which were particularly difficult to dislodge. At best it was a crooked hole. Undaunted, MacEwan noted that with better couplings it would bore a straighter well. The operators were making progress.

At the seven-metre level there was unexpected excitement. Alex and Bertha MacEwan were working late into the night and the boys were in bed when suddenly the well gave a rumbling sound. MacEwan's first thought was that it had to be natural gas. The two children awoke to both the strange noises coming from the well and their parents' instructions that nobody was to light a match. Questions arose about what the family would do if, indeed, they had a gas well. By morning, however, the rumbling had ceased and there was neither odour nor evidence of gas, which suited them just fine.

At the ten-metre level, the operators encountered water—not much, but enough to make mud. They were eager to give it a quality test. Again, the water was quite high in alkali, though the horses and cattle would drink it. Unless the MacEwan family wanted to use the water to make and sell Glauber's Salts, they would have to find better water. But the effort to drill the post-hole well was not over yet. MacEwan always refused to say a bad word about his friends and he was willing to give the inadequate well the benefit of the doubt, too. Indeed, it was MacEwan who suggested that if that well were enlarged to a normal well diameter, it would accumulate more water at its base and justify the heavy work of construction. His proposal was to devote the next winter to making the post-hole well into a square well with plank cribbing. He planned to construct a windlass that could haul the clay from the bottom of the well to the wellhead.

The project required two patient people, one working in the well, the other dumping buckets of clay at the top and sending the empties back down. One nice feature about the winter assignment was that working temperatures in the well were generally favourable. For the person working at the top of the well, however, conditions were just as commonly miserable.

To guard against cave-ins, the wooden cribbing was made in segments with the dimensions of a perfect cube, almost a metre on each surface with open ends, top and bottom, to give the hole continuity. As the hole got deeper, a new plank box with open top and bottom was fitted on top of the previous one, which was then slid down to the bottom of the deepening hole.

Once completed, the new well lived up to expectations. But the search continued over the years for an expanded water supply and many new wells were dug—some by hand, others bored by machinery to a depth of up to forty-five metres. Searching for groundwater, MacEwan often said, was a profitable experience until you had to pay the wages.

Not long ago, I had a chance to think about groundwater again when a friend phoned just before the season's first snowfall. He asked me if I would come out and "witch" a well on his farm, deep in southern Alberta. Surprised by the question, I immediately asked him why he had turned to me. "You belonged to a generation when every farm district had a witching expert or dowser," he replied. "I just figured you'd know something about it."

I admitted that long ago I had witched a few wells, slowly pacing over farmyards with a forked branch of green willow held out in front of me. Like other people, though, I could never prove whether my witching endeavours were a success or failure. Sure, I had seen landowners strike water where the wooden fork twisted in my hands, but I had also seen holes drilled that failed to agree with me. Consequently, I could not in all honesty claim much confidence in the water-finding value of the forked willow wand or twisted piece of barbed wire in my hands. There was never any doubt in my mind, however, about the presence of a force that caused the wand to pull or twist in certain places as if trying to give me a signal. It was easy to presume that I was getting a message about underground water just waiting to be tapped by a drilling machine.

In some areas, of course, it is necessary to drill to great depths to make a strike. In others it seems almost impossible to miss the water at shallower levels. This may call into question the widespread idea that underground water is confined to narrow channels or "streams." It is more likely that the given band of water exists over a broad area, meaning that if a strike of good water is made at the farm's kitchen door, the chances are favourable that a similar strike can be made at a pasture gate a short distance away.

I assured my friend that I would like to assist in his search for a promising well-site, just as long as he understood my reservations about the reliability of my witching. He said he understood and would not hold me responsible, even if he struck oil instead of water.

Perhaps nobody should be allowed to use a water witch unless he really believes in it. The old proverb says that "Faith without works is dead." Fair enough, but I would add that works without faith can be a dismal thing too, and nobody cares to be accused of debunking his own business. Personally, I hope that I will never outgrow the pleasure of both cutting a willow wand to search for a wayward vein of water, and listening to older witchers relate their experiences—stories no doubt embellished here and there.

Groundwater is an enduring mystery. In the past, the search for it elevated the water witcher to the status of a folk hero. It has hidden itself below the soils of the Canadian plains and nurtured those fortunate enough to find and tap it. Whether in underground streams or in pools deep below the surface, water not only tantalized the homesteader with the promise of its presence, but enriched his existence whenever he was lucky enough to tap its bounty with the help of either the water witcher, know-how or just plain good luck. In a vast land where productive soils bore grasses and crops that waved in the wind, the murky groundwater was an invisible partner, except of course to its seeker, who saw it as his salvation.

PART II: WATER'S PLACE
Chapter 1: The Blessing of Fresh Water

Thou visitest the earth and waterest it,
Thou greatly enrichest it;
The river of God is full of water;
Thou providest their grain,
For so thou has prepared it.
Thou waterest its furrows abundantly,
Settling its ridges, softening it with showers,
And blessing its growth.

—Psalm 65: 9&10

When Mother MacEwan announced that breakfast was ready, it meant that, regardless of lesser breakfast beverages like tea, coffee and skimmed milk, every place at the table had been served with a cup of clean water and a generous helping of multigrain porridge. If the farm hens were in a laying mood and there was a good trading market for eggs, our parents might have decided that they could afford the luxury of adding a few raisins to the porridge mix. Eaten with skimmed milk, buttermilk, molasses or brown sugar, the simple mixture

Mrs. Mary Boose drawing water from a well in Vulcan, Alberta c. 1910.
Pioneers had to dig deep to find essential clean water.
(Glenbow Museum Archives, NA-1462-2)

was a veritable nutritional panacea, to say nothing of the eating joy it afforded.

Nobody attacked their porridge until Mother MacEwan had said the blessing. Ninety years later, her words are still clear to me. Were she alive today, she would be greatly distressed by the growing absence of mealtime prayers of gratitude for clean water and sufficient food. Evening meals, with their more relaxed atmosphere, invited slightly longer table prayers and perchance some discussion about the wonder of water and its miraculous functions. "Oh, the wonder of it all," Mother would say. "What we have in our cups is the same stuff that halts the spread of deserts and the destructiveness of forest fires."

Mother's respect for clean water and her sympathy for those who did not have it explained her reverence for it and the ritual of the cup of water she placed at every porridge bowl. And miracles? Why, of course, they were all around us, especially where good clean water was a given fact. She took pains to explain to us that the vast bread-producing wheat fields drew their essential volumes of water from the snow and rain that fell in the mountains and plains. Water reached the crops by varying routes, and then most of it evaporated back to its place in the water cycle, thoroughly purified by light and heat for its next trip to the wheatlands.

When drawn into the subject of miracles, Mother MacEwan, who had been trained as a nurse, preferred examples furnished by the human body; she was especially fascinated by the wonders of appetite and digestion. She felt very strongly that Canadian children should be taught basic nutrition at public schools from grade four onwards. Thanks, she continued, should be offered in prayer for the related wonders of the body, which ensure a succession of physical-chemical wonders by which food is transformed in the stomach and intestines.

"We bring our humble thanks," our mother often said when all our heads were bowed, "for the nutritious food, our excellent appetites and amazing digestive systems that never rest and deserve our better understanding." We should talk more about the processes of the body, she would say, using common terms like protein, fat, carbohydrates, minerals and so on, each of which come under attack by the digestive juices. For her, the most difficult of all to comprehend was water. It accounted for most of our bodily makeup, yet left our bodies unchanged. Though it was polluted with various bodily wastes it was still, unalterably, water.

The grand circulation of water on the earth itself was another astonishing thing to ponder. If the water shuttling back and forth between clouds and the planet were capable of speech, one bubble might remark to another: "Take care of yourself until we pass again after a few more trips skyward to get cleaned up."

But seriously, I must say that we have no right to keep the great stories about the wonders of food and water to our-selves. Mother would have instructed that, "As beneficiaries, may God keep us grateful for our cups which overflow with pure water. But we must also be concerned for those many parts of the world which face almost constant food and water famine." In all moral fairness, I myself cannot deny at least some responsibility for my role as "Brother's Keeper." I must confess to feelings of guilt when I think of the world's vast deposits in silver and gold, oil and gas, and above all, water, and then consider how little we share the treasures of Nature to which no one of us has an exclusive claim. May we be pardoned for our refusal to share the rich harvests from the good soil, sunshine and water which are on loan to all of us.

Grant MacEwan at age two with his mother.
(MacEwan family archives)

Chapter Two: Water Is Everybody's Business

Everywhere, water is a thing of beauty, gleaming in the dew drops, singing in the summer rains, shining in the ice gems till the leaves all seem to turn to living jewels, spreading a gold veil over the setting sun or a white gauze around the midnight moon.

—John Ballantyne Gough

As a thirteen-year-old farm boy growing up at the beginning of the century, I had a very uncomplicated relationship with water. Water was wet stuff but it was all right to drink if you didn't have pop. It didn't have much taste unless it was dirty water from our pond and then it might make you sick, but it was all right for a bath. I didn't like taking baths too much, though. The water was always too hot or too cold, and I never failed to get soap in my eyes.

Water was tricky. If you put it in the kitchen kettle and heated it on the stove it turned to steam and disappeared. If it got awfully cold it turned to ice so hard you could skate on it. If you didn't have skates you just had to wait until spring to have your fun wading or swimming. My teacher told us every spring that if the water was deep and if we weren't good swimmers, we'd better not take our pants off.

But we were lucky to have water even though we couldn't swim. We heard at Sunday School that in some parts of the world many kids died from dirty water or from not having enough at all.

My little sister liked playing in the water too, so she could make mud pies. Before she was old enough to go to school it was my job to watch her and keep her from putting the mud in her mouth and trying to eat her pies. On wash days my mum would tell me to hurry home from school to help her carry water from the pond to her washtub where she let the dirty clothes soak overnight.

Water was puzzling and mysterious when I was growing up, but water is everybody's business—or should be. It is the foundation, the building block of life; without it, vast areas of country would be unproductive, supporting neither plant nor animal life. The human body's dependence on it is evidence of that as well. We begin as almost pure water. The human embryo is almost ninety percent water; during childhood, however, water content falls to roughly seventy-five percent of total body weight, and by adulthood has dropped to seventy percent or less. Still, to put it in perspective, a mature male weighing seventy-eight kilograms is carrying over forty-five kilograms of water, which, as a matter of routine, is a considerable burden at any time.

Water is absolutely crucial to our survival. If the human

body had managed to operate efficiently with less water, such a development would have occurred somewhere in the evolutionary process. Human beings can survive without food of the bread and butter kind for three weeks or more, but on rations totally without water they would be lucky to live much beyond two or three days. Every creature on earth requires water for various physical tasks, for which there are no substitutes. In mammals, water performs a wide range of physiological functions. It plays an important role in controlling and stabilizing body temperatures. Water also carries out such bodily chores as transporting glandular secretions, lubricating bone joints, furnishing extra moisture to areas such as the lungs, which need to be damp to function, and aiding in the removal of wastes from the urinary and intestinal systems.

Water is not like food constituents such as carbohydrates, proteins, fats and minerals, which yield to digestive juices and thereby furnish fuel for the generation of heat or energy, nor is it like protein, which is the building material for new body tissue. Water isn't broken down in the digestive process; however, the nutritional value of foods for humans and animals depends in large part on water content, or in more technical terms, "percentage of dry matter." Ripe fruits and some garden vegetables are more than half water or less than half dry matter. For instance, apples at picking time may be sixty-five percent water and if they are to be marketed as dry fruit will be processed to reduce their water content to around twenty-five percent. Ripe tomatoes will show water content as high as ninety-five percent, and the familiar potato a stunning eighty percent.

Water drawn into the stomach in food or liquid form is absorbed by the intestines to serve in a score of ways and, after fulfilling its function, is discharged as urine, perspiration or intestinal waste. However, it is capable of being reconditioned in Nature's great water cycle and returned to the earth, free of salt and other forms of body waste, to be used again and again.

Nature's magnificent water renewal (or hydrologic cycle) has been keeping the world's water on the move since long before the time of Noah, the Old Testament patriarch and captain of the most famous water craft, either legendary or real, in world story. The voyage saw members of Noah's family and two members, one male and one female, of every known animal species brought to a safe landing after forty long days. They sailed without benefit of propulsion, maps, and search and rescue services, and no more rules of the sea than pirates and rum runners would have heeded. And it may be fair to assume that the great Noah had no more knowledge of the fabulous hydrologic cycle than most water users of our present age.

Noah's adventure in flood water as told in the Book of Genesis may not be of much interest to scholars of modern science but it would be a mistake to ignore it entirely. One of the legacies from the Flood was the promise given to Noah that the waters would "never more become a flood to destroy all flesh" (Genesis 9:15). The descendents of Noah have been accused, perhaps not unfairly, of taking their rich gifts of water for granted. Their growing enthusiasm for water recreation and other uses has begun to change all that. North Americans love playing on and in the water. They eagerly fish in their favourite streams, and if health and age find them sufficiently fit, participate in water-related winter sports like skating, skiing, snow-shoeing, curling or hockey. A city realtor with many years of experience once remarked to this author that houses situated within walking distance of an ice rink or public swimming pool were the easiest ones to sell. "Show them the opportunity," he added, "and the older ones can still whoop, play and seek exercise like any sensible citizens."

Canadians tend to denounce snow shovels and heavy winter clothing, but it is an insensitive person who is not captivated by a pair of sundogs. Flirting with a feeble and bashful old sun, sundogs produce unbelievably lovely designs that look like geometric inventions crafted in crystal by angels.

In summer, people never become tired of the colourful beauty of the rainbow, or the massive works of water seen in the Grand Canyon or Niagara Falls—both water-carved national showpieces. In times past, many Canadians travelled great distances to spend at least part of their honeymoon at Niagara Falls, a ritual that was regarded more or less facetiously as a prerequisite to properly ordered matrimony. Although the Canadian Badlands in Alberta are not seen as a thing of wonder like the Grand Canyon, both are evidence of the spectacular work of water erosion. Both were among the first World Heritage sites to be chosen, and are enduring proof of the eroding power of the tireless and unshrinking waters of the mighty cycle for untold ages.

The role of water in recreation makes for a compelling story but it is water in industry that pays the dividends. Society in its upward movements has found a surprising number of new uses for water. In the flourishing years of the fur trade in the Canadian and American West, the main water-related industry was freighting on the bigger lakes and rivers, including the Mississippi and Missouri system in the United States, Canada's Saskatchewan and Mackenzie River systems, the Great Lakes, and the St. Lawrence River. Together they furnished a national network in Canada that invited canoes big and small, York Boats, and finally steamships with paddle wheels fuelled by wood salvaged from shorelines and crudely piled on their decks.

Considering again the relative economy of water transportation, it is tempting to suggest that stern wheels and paddle wheels may have been retired too soon and allowed to disappear in Canada, particularly in the West. A bigger share of local and semi-local freight might have been left to the rivers and lakes as it was in Europe and the United States. Instead of overbuilding railroads, it would have been more efficient to build waterways as junior partners in national transportation. Unfortunately, the idea of giving waterways a permanent role was allowed to be forgotten very early, and has now, in many cases, been rendered unfeasible by the construction of low bridges, dams and weirs. There were some proposals, for instance, to recover the navigational potential of the Saskatchewan River in the early twentieth century but the additional cost of reconstructing numerous bridges discouraged development.

Meanwhile, sawmills and grist mills offered compelling challenges to individuals dreaming of the wood fuel, raw materials, and water power that were waiting to be brought together in industry. The day came when water became essential to industry: hydro-electric power lines to the mills made sawing, gristing and the like much easier and faster, and spelled the fortunes of many entrepreneurs.

Many are unaware of how water is used in Canada. In the present state of industry, almost half the water drawn from natural supplies is used in the generation of thermal power. Next comes the manufacturing sector with its enormous appetite for water: eighteen barrels of water are required to refine one barrel of oil, while a big paper mill requires as much water every day as a medium-sized city. Then there is the volume of water needed to meet various municipal and domestic purposes. Coming after all of these is the water required for agriculture and irrigation.

American environmentalists have often reminded us of the sins of omission. It may be that they are correct in criticizing Canadians for their lacklustre efforts in cultivating a better understanding of their water resources. Adults as well as children, they have said, should be encouraged to indulge in the simple exercise of enumerating and assessing the countless uses of the nation's water.

For the first of such exercises, this author looks back with awe and admiration to an excellent public school teacher in one of Prairie Canada's one-room country schools. The teacher in question, Olive Durnin, presided with dignity and unquestioned authority over the mixed classroom population of between twenty to fifty pupils. (The number depended on the season of the year and the need for more helpers on the farms). Pupil ages ranged from six years to twenty-six. Her attention was often needed in at least eight directions at once, and it is safe to presume that when she walked to her living quarters at the end of the day, feelings of guilt for being over-paid were not among her worries.

In 1915, Olive Durnin was my teacher at Spry School, ten kilometres south of Melfort, Saskatchewan. Memories can play strange tricks on us, especially ones compiled over the course of ninety-odd years. However, my conviction remains as strong as ever that she was one of the first in Western Canada to place an emphasis in the classroom on soil, trees, and water. An educational dynamo, she firmly piloted an important venture in introducing environmentalism into the school curriculum. One of the first things she had us do was enumerate water's many different uses. Here are some of the wide-ranging uses we students came up with:

1. Water of good quality keeps humans and animals, wild and tame, alive and well.
2. Water meets other farm needs like irrigation of crops.
3. Water accommodates various other household require-ments like cooking, washing and bathing.
4. Municipalities bring roadway dust under control by spraying the offending travel routes with water and get-ting the same relief as could be expected from a light fall of rain.
5. Water is the basic ingredient in fire fighting around the world.

What Olive Durnin reinforced in her teaching was that nothing should be considered a substitute for clear, unadulter-ated water. Encouraging Canadians to drink plenty of water every day might use up roughly five billion litres a day which, when spread over the nation, would not present much of a problem. It may seem contradictory to encourage North Americans to drink a few additional glasses of water a day while at the same time hoping to share the North American good-water fortune with those in need in other parts of the world. The obstacles to transporting a product as bulky and unwieldy as water over great global distances seem to defy all that is practical, leaving too many Canadians to conclude that it cannot happen in the foreseeable future. Eager and generous North Americans must try to find some other means of sharing their prosperity, perhaps by financing more desalination plants for their distant neighbours, and then feeling somewhat better about consuming those additional glasses of water. Good water can be put to a thousand different uses but the greatest of these will continue to be in providing drinking water for humans and animals.

Medicine Lake, Jasper: "the unending circulation of the earth's moisture and water."
(D. Shawn Kabatoff / Vision Images)

Chapter Three: The Amazing Cycle of World Water

The unending circulation of the earth's moisture and water is called the water cycle. It is a gigantic system, operating in and on the land and oceans of the earth, and in the atmosphere that surrounds it.

—William C. Ackermann

It's a watery old world, or so the maps make it appear. Water occupies almost twice as much of the world's surface as dry land. Of course, most of the exposed water is oceanic and high in suspended salt, making it quite unsuitable for consumption by humans or animals. It is too salty for irrigation of crops and is of limited use even for manufacturing operations. What maps of the earth's surface reveal about water distribution could be misleading without the recognition of the vital importance of water quality.

The fact that ninety-seven percent of the world's water is in the oceans may give satisfaction to sailors and fishermen but leaves a large part of the world's inhabitants still searching for acceptable drinking water. The quantity of fresh water on the earth and the distribution of it often leaves much to be desired, taxing the imaginations of conservationists and water specialists who face the constant challenge of making existing supplies go further.

Up to three-and-a-half percent of seawater consists of chlorides like magnesium chloride or sodium chloride which we know as table salt. The abundance of salt water has prompted people interested in the quality of the world's drinking water to lament bitterly that three-quarters of the world's fresh water is locked away in the glaciers and polar icecaps. The inevitable consequence is that available fresh water amounts to only about one percent of the world's overall water total. If a just complaint about Nature's allocations is sought, this might be the place to find it. As it is, that coveted fresh water is most likely to be found in streams, lakes and existing wells, leaving humans with perpetual stewardship and searching duties.

The population of the world continues to grow at an ever-accelerating rate. With over six billion souls on the earth, fresh water supplies are already being tested to the limit. If human beings and their fellow creatures are to survive, nothing looms larger than the need for better safeguards for tomorrow's supplies of water. Even the best conservation programme is not likely to reverse the imbalance in natural distribution exacerbated by human ignorance. Human indifference has been a leading enemy and water has suffered as a result. Those who have laid claim to the water are learning and three great truths have emerged: to pollute is easy, but is both lunatic and sinful; to rehabilitate water is possible, but is slow and costly; and to destroy it is utterly impossible.

If water had an exact point of origin it would be with the chemical elements hydrogen and oxygen, both of which are gases in their purest state. When an atom of oxygen and two atoms of hydrogen come together, they form the simple molecule, H_2O, the chemical formula for water. One of water's distinctive qualities is its ability to take the form of a solid, a vapour, or a liquid. In its pure state, it is tasteless, colourless and odourless. Normally it freezes and becomes a solid (ice) at 0° Centigrade, and boils and vapourizes at 100° Centigrade. Fortunately a person does not require an understanding of advanced chemistry to appreciate water's makeup.

Water should inspire sweet songs of praise as the earth's circulating masterpiece. Call it what you like, the hydrologic cycle, or simply Nature's mighty water wheel, it is the biggest clean-up show on earth, played out in the clouds, fields, streams, lakes, and deep beneath the surface of the planet. A rural philosopher once said that Nature could drop thirty centimetres of water on his farmland with less noise and complaint than is usually heard from his hired man after taking a dose of castor oil.

The movement of water within the hydrologic cycle can take many different routes. Rain falling upon the ocean will quickly become salty, and will gradually evaporate into the atmosphere where it will meet the cycle's needs in the days ahead. The precipitation that falls on land will serve exactly the same purpose, but will take a more roundabout course in furnishing the vapour needed in the atmosphere. Falling as either rain or snow, it will penetrate the ground or become runoff. If it soaks into the ground it will gradually add to the groundwater supply, where it may sit for thousands of years before slowly moving on. It may then enter an underground water course before draining into an aquifer or stream to blend with a larger stream. Or the rain may fall on a lake and go from there to a river flowing to an ocean where it will become part of the world's largest body of water. It will then evaporate from the surface of the ocean to the atmosphere to await some particles of dust around which drops of water will form. Eventually the water will plummet earthward as rain to start the turn of the water wheel all over again.

How many times has a given molecule of water made the long journey through the complete hydrologic cycle? It would take a wild guess to answer such a question, but it might need to be measured in thousands of years. It is sufficient for the student of water to know that the hydrologic cycle has never been known to break down. Its typical performance has been "slow but sure," uncertain in its scheduling but unfailing in its purpose. The world's water is still abundant, but is neither more nor less abundant than when the Vikings landed on North American shores a thousand years ago. It may grow more difficult to manage but it never wears out.

The movements of the cycle are, of course, disrupted by a great variety of human uses. It generally takes thirteen litres of water to flush a toilet, thirty litres to wash the dinner dishes, 110 litres to fill a bathtub, nine litres a minute for a shower, and 450 litres to wash the family car. All of these activities benefit from the often unrecognized cleansing effects of the water cycle. What the users of that water forget is the tragedy that would result if they had to live with their dirty water without restoration, or had no steady supply of fresh water to turn to. Scientists realized early on in the study of the water cycle that the world's water is of a fixed quantity, unchanging from year to year, and they began to wonder how much of that precious resource exists. Researchers were organised to measure the amounts of water falling as rain or snow, and the volume of water flowing from rivers as they discharged into lakes or oceans. They then wondered whether to attempt the more difficult task of ascertaining, at least approximately, the total world supply of water at whatever point it may be in the cycle. The resulting estimates were much contested, but the figure of 1.4 billion cubic kilometres has become widely accepted. It is an incomprehensibly enormous figure that enlarged rather than diminished previous estimates of the cycle's magnitude.

If the planet's total water supply were equally distributed, the amount for each man, woman and child would far exceed their need. And yet many still face the threat of shortages of good drinking water. Concerned citizens dare not relax their emphasis on water of drinking quality. If there is not enough good water, the challenge must be nothing less than conversion to drinking water of the required amounts. It is a process which is technologically feasible today, and will become an inescapable necessity in the future.

The hydrologic cycle is a recycling waterworks on a scale that is far too big and at the same time too efficient for human comprehension. Yet it is there for everybody, young and old, rich or poor. And for every person who recognizes the magnitude, importance and the majesty of water and the great cycle into which it is locked, may there be an equally eager desire to sing songs of praise. If it were left to the author of these lines to select a theme song for this book, the choice would fall upon an ageless hymn "O Wondrous God, When I Thy World Consider (How Great Thou Art)":

When in the storm I hear the voice of thunder,
And lightning flashes swift across the sky;
When cold fresh winds blow in across the water,
And rainbows glisten bright before my eyes;
Then soars my soul in joyful songs of praise,
O wondrous God, how great Thou art!

May praise for good water and the precious gifts of soil and forests and clean air be joyously sounded.

PART III: MOVING WATER
Chapter Four: Water Flowing Into Hudson's Bay

One may love a river as soon as one sets eyes on it. It may have certain features that fit instantly with one's conception of beauty, or it may recall the qualities of some other river, well known and deeply loved. One may feel in the same way an instant affinity for a man or a woman and know that here is pleasure and warmth and the foundation of a deep friendship. In either case, the full riches of the discovery are not immediately released—they cannot be; only knowledge and close experience can release them. One cannot know intimately all the ways and movement of a river without growing to love it.
—Roderick L. Haig-Brown,
A River Never Sleeps, 1944.

Everything fashioned for the northern part of North America seems tailor-made according to an especially large pattern. It is most clearly the case with Nature's water reserves of both fresh and salt

The York Factory was the final conquest in the battle between the
French and the English to claim Hudson's Bay. c. 1882.
(From an illustration in "Picturesque Canada"
Glenbow Museum Archives, NA-1041-7)

water in this vast region. The biggest spectacle in all of the North is Hudson's Bay, with its 650,000 square kilometres of salt water. One of the most common disappointments associated with the Bay was that it never lived up to its potential as a short and reliable water route to the fabled treasures and markets of the Far East. As northern history unfolded, however, the Bay became the most economical route for the fur trade, both in carrying raw furs to world markets, and in importing trade goods such as guns, ammunition, tobacco, alcoholic beverages, beads, woollen clothing and much more. The Hudson's Bay Company, depending on the monopolistic privileges granted by its Royal Charter, used the Bay route almost exclusively, and the North West Company might have done the same had its rival made the route available.

In due course, the same shipping lanes through the Bay proved most suitable for immigrants like the Selkirk settlers of 1812 and those who came later. An extremely slow journey by sailing vessel, it could take up to six months to make the crossing from Europe and required more months when it became necessary to break the trip by wintering near York Factory or Fort Prince of Wales. With the pioneer use of the Bay for trade and travel into Rupert's Land, the sea route to the port at York Factory gained widespread use. Halifax and Montréal offered the best transatlantic travel for those passengers whose destinations were near the eastern seaport, but they could not compete for inland destinations like Fort Garry or Fort Edmonton.

Even the earliest immigrants to make their way to the West after the passage of the Dominion Lands Act in 1872 believed they should demand nothing less than a rail connection between the prairie country and some point on the western shore of Hudson's Bay. By such a route, they argued, ocean-going ships could be economically loaded with grain for the remainder of the trip by water to the consumer markets of Europe or elsewhere. The demands for a Hudson's Bay Railway grew to be the hottest political issue in Prairie Canada. For at least forty years after 1880, every farm convention held in the Canadian West was asked to entertain a resolution calling on the government of Canada to take steps to establish the rail line.

It was widely recognized that the Montréal business community would be opposed to any amount of export grain bypassing the Port of Montréal by way of Hudson's Bay. Montréal's political influence was ultimately ignored during the federal election campaign of 1908, which Prime Minister Wilfrid Laurier was particularly anxious to win. While he probably recognized that any policies with respect to the future of the Hudson's Bay Railroad were politically hazardous, he appreciated the necessity of taking a firm stand. Accordingly, he announced during a campaign speech at Niagara Falls on September 18, 1908, that if his government were elected, it would undertake the construction of the Hudson's Bay Railway.

The proposal was happily received in the West. After Laurier's Liberals did indeed win the election, however, the Ottawa administration was slow in acting, anticipating opposition from Montréal. Western farmers grew impatient and more vocal. "We've waited long enough," said the Grain Grower's

Guide of 1911. "Let's build the railway ourselves. We can pay for it while waiting for the Government to act." The sustained protests from the farmers shook Ottawa into some form of concerted action. The first decision to be made was the choice of a port. The merits of both Nelson and Churchill were placed before eminent English engineer Frederick Palmer. After weighing the advantages of Nelson and Churchill at the mouths of their respective rivers, Palmer opted for the latter. Work began on the rail link to the port and proceeded somewhat slowly. Finally, on March 29, 1929, Ottawa received a triumphant telegram: "STEEL REACHED CHURCHILL TODAY."

The ocean-going vessels Farnsworth and Warkworth, two tramp steamers from Newcastle-On-Tyne, came to Churchill for grain in 1931. Ten ships came in 1932 and loaded a total of 2.7 million bushels of grain into their holds. It was encouraging but too soon for rejoicing. Marine insurance for the passage was prohibitively high and the shipping season short—roughly three months. Then disaster struck. On October 1, 1932, the freighter, Bright Fan, carrying a quarter of a million bushels of wheat in her holds, struck an iceberg at the entrance to Hudson's Strait and, in short order, plunged to the sea bottom. Fortunately, there was no loss of life, but northern shipping never fully recovered from that blow.

There have been good and poor years for northern shipping in the sixty-five years of freighting on Hudson's Bay since the shipwreck of the Bright Fan. The Hudson's Bay Railway to dockside at Churchill still finds many loyal supporters who would argue quite vehemently that a country like Canada, with such an extensive northern coastline, needs a port in those reaches. Nevertheless, the grand hopes for the port have in many ways failed to become a reality.

Hudson's Bay, to the surprise of many Canadians, is important in the history of the Ice Age as well as in the exploration and fur trade periods. Just as Nova Scotia, for example, has strong links to Scotland and France, so western Canada has equally strong ties to the traditions of the northern indigenous peoples. Even today, scholars and tourists may find undisturbed gravel beaches that tell of Hudson's Bay when it was a freshwater sea, several times its present size and created by the meltwater from Ice Age glaciers so thick and heavy that they twisted the earth's crust. Not far away from those beaches, the student of North American history may inspect sites and structures that were part of York Factory when it functioned as the headquarters of the extensive trade in furs operating out of Hudson's Bay. And slightly further north is the site where an intriguing naval battle between imperial France and England was fought to determine supremacy over the Bay in August 1697.

Nobody at that time expected to hear of an important naval battle being fought by two of Europe's strongest powers for mastery of the remote waters of Hudson's Bay. The "Gentlemen Adventurers of England trading into the Hudson's Bay" were quite satisfied with Charles II's Royal Charter, which granted them the trade monopoly over Rupert's Land in 1670. True, the English were the first Europeans to claim the Bay on the strength of Henry Hudson's discovery of it by sea. But the French argued that their people were the first Europeans to see the Bay from the south or overland side, thereby giving them the primary claim. Moreover, the French contended that, just as Charles II had conveyed handsome land grants with his Charter, Louis XIII had in 1628 made similar land grants to the French "Company of One Hundred Associates."

The first major French assault on the Hudson's Bay Company positions in the Bay may have been when Chevalier de Troyes, in 1686, led a hundred soldiers and volunteers on a thousand-kilometre expedition by foot and canoe to the south end of James Bay. There he attacked and captured the English company's trading posts on the Moose, Rupert and Albany Rivers, leaving the company with only one location on the Bay, York Factory.

The inconvenience of warfare without a formal declaration of war continued for years, right up to the signing of the Treaty of Utrecht in 1713. In the meantime, the French and English continued their attempts to claim Hudson's Bay through raids and insults. The inevitable showdown occurred on September 5, 1697. Four French ships were on their way towards York Factory under the command of Pierre Iberville. They entered Hudson's Strait and were immediately caught in heavy ice, losing communication with each other. Iberville's flagship, the Pélican, was the first to free itself but he was unable to locate his other ships. Assuming that they were also free of the ice, he decided, quite reasonably, to sail on and hoped to regroup before reaching York Factory on the mouth of the Nelson River.

Coming within sight of York Factory, the French captain rejoiced to see three ships at anchor in the estuary. He soon realized they were not his ships at all, but rather three British vessels, two frigates and the warship, Hampshire. Iberville knew he was in a bad position with few options open to him. Very simply, he could either fight or run. For a man with a fine reputation and unusual skill in naval manoeuvres, his decision should not be too surprising. Iberville decided to fight, despite the poor odds. Observers would have said he was in trouble. Indeed, somebody was in trouble but it was not Iberville. Finding the Hampshire broadside, he was able to launch a short-range volley; the mortally wounded man-of-war rolled over and sank, taking 290 men to an icy grave. One of the remaining frigates became lost in the ice and ultimately surrendered to Iberville. The other fled to the Nelson River. The French flag was raised on York Factory, and its name changed to Fort Bourbon. The subsequent Treaty of Utrecht in 1713, however, dramatically reversed these temporary French gains. This treaty, signed on the other side of the Atlantic, was to ensure the permanency of the English presence in Hudson's Bay.

Not unlike these shifts in the balance of imperial power, Nature's distribution of stream water with good potential for hydro-electric generation is far from equitable, and countries have not always done much to correct this deficiency. In Canada, the provinces of Quebec and British Columbia inherited the largest and best resources for water power. Prince Edward Island, on the other hand, where one is at pains to find a mountain or a river, has virtually none. Most Canadian provinces and territories have been richly blessed with gifts of water capable of being used to generate power. At the beginning of the present century Canada generated 173,000 horsepower by that means. In 1962, that figure had risen to almost twenty-seven million horsepower, with much more power still unharnessed.

The exceptional potential of Quebec's water power resources had long been recognized. It was not until after the Second World War that serious consideration was given to their development. The birth of the James Bay project came after the ferment that marked Quebec's political scene in the 1960s. Jean Lesage, leader of the Liberal Party, fought a provincial election in 1962 on the rights of public ownership of all electric utilities. His decisive victory set a new political tone. As time was to demonstrate, however, one danger lay in moving too fast.

The memorable René Lévesque, an early member of Lesage's Liberal government, held the cabinet portfolio for Water Resources. When his ambition was channelled into the formation and leadership of the Sovereignty Association in 1968, he took with him his own clear vision as to what course the development of Quebec's water potential should take. One mistake in addressing Quebec's water programmes at the time was an announcement of the gigantic James Bay Project by a member of the provincial government in 1971, before the Cree people living in the area had been notified of the scheme. It took four more years of negotiations to remedy the misunderstanding, but by 1975 the Cree people largely supported the project.

Cynics said that the pursuit of a settlement did not matter because the big project would not succeed anyway. The First

Nations peoples had come to understand the white man's way of "sharing" resources with the original residents. They said: "He'll never settle for any terms except his own." But under René Lévesque's influence, the final agreement between First Nations peoples and others produced a settlement with an unexpected measure of justice. Each tribe or group saw assurance of hunting and fishing in perpetuity, land grants, payment for the removal of dead wood from areas flooded by dams, availability of wood needed by residents for any purpose, education for native children, medical services, a degree of self-government and even cash allowances under certain circumstances. It was a triumph for James Bay relations, and one far beyond the expectations of native groups.

What of costs and funding for anything so stupendous as the James Bay Project? They were staggering, like the vast bay itself. Government sources reported costs of $21 billion in the late 1970s, though unconfirmed sources said it could be closer to $30 billion. The huge loans taken out to finance the project may have bothered many people, but there was comfort in the thought that the taxpayers of Quebec were making an investment that would pay immeasurable dividends in the long run.

Chapter Five: Water Carrying Freight

A convention consisting of delegates of the Boards of Trade and other such bodies in Canada and the United States will be held at Duluth, [Minnesota], August 15 [1882], for the purpose of considering the proposition to connect the Red River with Lake Superior by means of a canal....The value and importance of the canal to the prairie Province cannot be questioned.

—Winnipeg World Times, August 2, 1882.

It was the hope for improved water transportation that induced the earliest Canadian interest in canals in Upper Canada and the Maritime provinces. Surface water was widespread, but in most instances it seemed the main supply was in the wrong places, or flowing in inconvenient directions. As the landowners saw it, the wild water was about as rebellious and undisciplined as a killer whale entangled in a fish net. Clearly, the challenge was to make the water serviceable for boating or other purposes, as the Americans had done with the Mississippi River.

The Sternwheeler "Midnight Sun" on the Athabasca River: improved water routes allowed the transportation of supplies on rivers and waterways.
(Glenbow Museum Archives, NA-1338-14)

Canadian interest came a little later but with an enthusiasm that saw many Canadian operators acquiring canal boats before they had canals.

Where small canals were constructed, the work advanced at a speed that suited the capacity of local citizens. Any person possessing good pioneer muscle, a wheelbarrow and a digging spade could start moving earth and rocks at short notice. All work in connection with canal construction was slow and tedious and few of the many ditches begun were ever completed to give their builders the joy of dispatching a shipment of cured pork to Winnipeg, or wheat to St. Paul, or anything edible to Norway House or Port Churchill.

The major problems in pioneer rafting or boating without propulsion lay in the freighting hazards of Niagara Falls, the Lachine Rapids on the St. Lawrence River, the lower ends of the Saskatchewan River, and a score of other dangerous straits. The wild Lachine gave the impression of a crusty old man constantly close to anger. Even explorers with the courage and drive of a Jacques Cartier had second thoughts about continuing their search for the Northwest Passage or a route to the Orient by way of the unruly river. The search did not end, however, and the spectacular scale of the construction along the Lachine was to be seen in the following years as among the most memorable in Canadian canal-building history.

It is noteworthy that arbitration won a double triumph for canals in 1821. The two old fur trading companies that had long held monopoly advantages in the trading of fur in Rupert's Land—the Hudson's Bay Company of English origin based in London and the North-West Company of highland

Scottish origin, headquartered in Montréal—managed to settle their differences and amalgamated under the name of the English company. The new company, by inheriting the Royal Trading Charter that had been conferred initially upon the Hudson's Bay Company, peaceably ensured a long-held trading monopoly. It then became easier for Upper and Lower Canada to forget their greedy quarrels and co-operate in dealing with the St. Lawrence River canals.

The first major canal on the Lachine was completed for use in 1825, and the proudly-acclaimed Welland Canal on the Niagara River followed about four years later. The new spirit of co-operation made it easier to obtain either public or private funds for such big enterprises. In design and operations the Welland was a proper companion for the Lachine, but because of its proximity to the world-famous Niagara Falls and its working relationship with it, the Welland became better known. The first Welland was completed in 1829 to allow ships to bypass the wild Niagara River and formidable Niagara Falls, and accommodate the widely different water levels, a variant of almost a hundred metres between Lakes Erie and Ontario.

Another canal soon joined the Lachine and Welland as an object of widespread Canadian pride. The Rideau Canal, built between 1826 and 1832 and incorporating fifty dams and almost as many locks, was conceived as a military necessity. About two hundred kilometres long, it was envisioned to furnish a defending army with an alternative and safer route between the Ottawa River, where Ottawa stands today, and Kingston on Lake Ontario.

Every engineering structure with the monumental proportions of a Welland or a Rideau needed an engineering super-man, and these Canadian projects had them. Behind the Welland was William Hamilton Merritt of St. Catharines, and behind the Rideau was Lieutenant Colonel John By. For the latter, the work camp and headquarters were located beside the Ottawa River, a spot that became known as Bytown, and still later, Ottawa.

The hardship of digging and moving soil in that period should not be forgotten. Much of the region staked for canals was hardwood bush country from which the removal of big trees and massive roots was a formidable task even before the first cartload of earth and stones was moved. And when soil and clay had to be loosened, loaded, and unloaded, the best and only means in most cases was the time-tested spade and shovel. For the horses and oxen used for moving the loaded carts, the work was nothing short of gruelling.

Most but not all of Canada's historic canals have now fallen into disuse. Some have continued to play traditional roles. Visitors to Ottawa see the highly-respected Rideau being used in both summer and winter for extremely popular recreation, making it easy for citizens of Ottawa to "love their Rideau."

Like the Maritimers, the people in Western Canada had limited stream water to utilize. They had great rivers like the Mackenzie, which was named in honour of Alexander Mackenzie, who in 1789 paddled to its mouth and realized, to his great disappointment, that he was looking at the Arctic rather than the Pacific Ocean. (Mackenzie, who was later knighted, tried again and was successful in reaching the Pacific by land). Of the West's other great rivers, there was the Fraser, to which British Columbia had almost exclusive claim, as well as the Peace, and the Red. The broad Saskatchewan system was particularly important for the fur trade and, like the Mackenzie, took its water northward to spill into the Arctic.

In other words, the West had a few great rivers but they did not always flow in directions useful to industry and commerce. Nonetheless, the region has seen a long evolution of transportation by water; from small canoes and big freight canoes called York boats, to some strange-looking contraptions called steamboats. The first of the steamboats—named the "Anson Northup" after her proprietor and captain—was said to look like a raft carrying a farmer's coal shed and was equipped with a steam-driven paddle wheel at the stern. The ship's first appearance on the Red River at Fort Garry was on a bright day in June 1859, and Fort Garry residents, hearing the toots from the steamer's whistle, rushed to the river to see the boat for themselves.

The ship's story up to that time had been anything but distinguished. It had been in service hauling freight on the Mississippi when Northup heard that the Board of Trade at St. Paul, anxious to attract Fort Garry's trade in freight—mostly furs and buffalo hides— was offering a thousand-dollar reward to the first owner of a steamboat who would take the ship to Fort Garry. Enticed by the reward, he bought this old wreck, cut it into three pieces, and hauled them overland from the Mississippi to Moorhead on the Upper Red River. He then reassembled the boat and steamed down the Red to Fort Garry to qualify for the Board of Trade's prize. The ship was scheduled to make a round trip as far as Moorhead every ten days, but it soon had competition from other steamboats on the river. By 1875, it was reported that Winnipeg's freight traffic on the Red River totalled 35,000 tonnes, a shift that crippled the traditional overland trade by Red River cart. The West's expanding merchant marine soon carried passengers and freight along the Assiniboine Rivers and Lake Winnipeg, and eventually steamers plied the Saskatchewan River as far as Fort Edmonton. The steamship service was welcomed, of course, but it could do little to overcome the excessively high cost of shipping wheat and livestock and other goods over great distances to market. Many westerners bemoaned the lack of a satisfactory water route to Liverpool or Montréal. The response was a suggestion that western interests should band together to dig their own canals much as easterners had dug theirs. The idea gained popularity and a meeting was called to assemble at Duluth, Minnesota, in August 1882. The Manitoba Daily Free Press, though, had slight reservations:

> *The enterprising people of Duluth are trying to revive public interest in a project first noted ten or eleven years ago to connect the waters of Lake Superior at that city with that of Red River at Grand Forks by means of a canal... It is claimed that the Canadian North-West, and Winnipeg in particular, would be greatly benefited by the canal, that, in fact, it would form a complete outlet with the Canadian Pacific Railway for the*

> *trade of the Northwest, and that it is therefore*
> *the self-interest of our people to aid in promot-*
> *ing it... By constructing only thirty-seven miles*
> *of actual canal, fifty-six dams and 111 locks at a*
> *total cost of $3,800,000 and utilizing the inter-*
> *vening natural waterways it is considered that*
> *nearly 4,000 miles [6,400 kilometres] of lakes*
> *and river navigation in the United States and*
> *Canada would be open... However, owing to*
> *the tortuous routes of the river to be navigated*
> *there is some reason to doubt.*

The Duluth scheme did not survive to see any earth being moved, but by 1905 the interest of the region was captured by the Georgian Bay Canal proposal. It would have seen western grain taken from the Great Lakes at about Parry Sound on Georgian Bay, and sent east via river and canal routes to Lake Ontario, thereby shortening the freight delivered via the Welland Canal route by about 1,500 kilometres. Proponents claimed the grain shipped by such a route would reach the Atlantic tidewater from the Great Lakes seventy-five hours earlier than by way of the Welland Canal and St. Lawrence River. The editor of the Farmer's Advocate in Winnipeg made the further observation that the time-saving would mean an economy of three days of inland navigation each way, and would be applicable to the commerce of over 360,000 square kilometres of North America.

Another scheme brought forward in 1906 sought to solve the problem of a link between the Great Lakes and Hudson's

Bay. A phenomenally ambitious proposal, it would have involved creating a navigable waterway over the vast distance from Lake Superior to James Bay by way of the Nipigon River. The idea faced many insurmountable challenges, the main one being that the route was hardrock country all the way, and never got off the ground.

Ironically, an answer of sorts to the Western Canadian dream of water routes to enhance commerce was found, not in the wild and wonderful waterways of the Canadian Shield or interior plains, but in tropical jungles half a continent away. Westerners applauded the opening of the sixty-five kilometre Panama Canal in 1914. In enabling the westward movement of grain and other goods, the long-awaited canal meant a shift away from reliance on traditional but costly eastern routes to world markets.

A vivid example of erosion caused by heavy rains. Kneehill Valley, Alberta.
(Glenbow Museum Archives, NA-2251-14)

Chapter Six: Erosion and Beauty

At least three billion tons of solid soil materials are washed out of the fields and pastures of the United States each year by water erosion alone. It has been figured that to move such a bulk of American soil on rails would take a train of freight cars 475,000 miles [766,000 kilometres] long, long enough to girdle the planet eighteen times at the equator. —Lord Russell, 1955

Each of the world's great rivers can offer fair reasons to boast, but nobody can blame the Americans who have seen to it that their favourite river has received inordinate praise. Canada, too, has its mighty rivers which continue to inspire pride, such as the Mackenzie, the St. Lawrence, or the Fraser. Still, it has none to rate with the Amazon, Mississippi, Ganges-Brahmaputra, Yellow, or Nile. Every person deeply interested in water should have an appreciative understanding of these rivers, including the problems of erosion that are associated with them.

If you question the citizens of any community, they will likely reveal their true feelings of affection and loyalty for one particular lake or stream. For the author of this book it is one from his boyhood years: the delightful East River in Nova Scotia's Pictou County where a revered grandfather washed his sheep before shearing them, and where I was encouraged to believe that I was an important part of the operation. Certainly, a great percentage of citizens of the United States hold the Mississippi in high regard. It has the distinction of being one of the longest rivers in the world, the one with the broadest drainage basin, the one with the most versatile system of navigation services and, to cap it all, the one with the richest body of river lore (much of it owing to Mark Twain) built up around it. Canadians should not be entirely jealous because a short section of the Missouri-Mississippi system, a spectacular canyon and all, winds its way through southern Alberta as the Milk River.

A few Canadians have had the temerity to observe that the Mississippi's discoverer was a Canadian, or at least a traveller from parts that became Canada: the great French explorer, René-Robert Cavelier de la Salle. It was twelve years after Charles II of England had granted exclusive trading privileges in all the North American territory draining into Hudson's Bay to the new Hudson's Bay Company. La Salle, as if trying to escape the influence of the Hudson's Bay Company, took leave from French Canada in 1682 to paddle down the big river that the native peoples said flowed to salt water.

According to legend, La Salle made that noted journey at his own expense. In any case, he knew why he was there, and at Louisiana he erected a huge wooden cross that claimed the region for his king, Louis XIV of France. Doubtless the ambitious explorer wanted to bestow a French name on the big river, but his career was cut short by his murder in 1687 while he was still occupied with founding a colony at the river's mouth. Of course there is nothing wrong with the river's Algonquin name, Mississippi, aside from its tricky spelling. It means "Father of Rivers" or "Father of Many Waters," which in the light of its many tributaries is highly appropriate.

At the Mississippi's northern point of origin, a tiny stream called the Ipasco flows from a tiny lake. Sometimes four metres in width, it is shallow enough to allow parents and children to wade without wetting their knees. As the river rolls south from the small lake, it will never be this slight again. Its volume increases with the repeated inflow of tributary waters along the way, making it the central pillar in the American river transportation system. Many large rivers drain into the Mississippi, including the Missouri, Illinois, Ohio, Arkansas and southern Red. All of these are major rivers in their own right and of supreme benefit in giving the United States the reputation of having the most efficient river navigation system in the world. Having safeguarded twenty-five thousand kilometres of inland water courses for future use is a praiseworthy American accomplishment. Compared with air, rail and highway transport, water transportation is slow and old-fashioned, but it is likely to survive as the most economical way of moving certain goods. Having protected its watercourses for so many years, the United States will never totally abandon river freight.

During his time as the chief of Soil Conservation in Washington, Dr. Hugh H. Bennett, widely known as "Big Hugh," declared that 50,000 acres of United States cropland had been lost by water and wind erosion, and another 50,000 acres "almost" lost. How much of that loss of a priceless resource had been directly due to the eroding forces of the Mississippi River nobody was sure.

It has been recently reported from Washington that the great Mississippi River, with its two million square kilometres of drainage basin, continues to draw unsuspected amounts of silt and sand and humus from its countless tributaries. Between 200 and 300 million tonnes of soil are being carried past the city of New Orleans every year. To put those figures into perspective, the soil equivalent of a twenty-acre field to plow depth—meaning about twelve centimetres—passes the city every hour of every day. This lost soil makes its new and perhaps permanent home on the floor of the Gulf of Mexico or Atlantic Ocean where it is neither wanted nor needed.

The large rivers are the first to be blamed by the public as evil soil robbers simply because they are completely without conscience and make no apology for lifting the biggest possible share of the precious soil treasure. A river that is running full can cause heavy erosion damage but even a relatively small volume of water moving downhill after a heavy rain can strip the land and leave ugly and wasteful scars. The practical fact is that soil loses its stability in the presence of water and loses it faster in the presence of running water. The forces of erosion, however, are not necessarily in a hurry; the erosion that produced the Grand Canyon in the northwestern region of the Arizona badlands must have scored the highest rating for patient persistence.

Until the adoption of simple and reliable methods for measuring water flow in streams and rivers, our understanding of the dynamics of erosion was largely guess work. At that time there was little hope of raising riverside debate above the folksy, Huckleberry Finn level.

After the Second World War, a controlled experiment was conducted at the federal Experimental Farm in Ottawa in response to the growing interest in soil erosion. A one-acre plot on a ten percent hillside grade was planted with cornrows following the steepest grade. It was the wrong way to plant corn, but it was a good way to demonstrate the destructive results of a heavy runoff. In a situation like this, the sand and the gravel remained behind, but the topsoil with its precious plant food had almost vanished, and the total loss of solid matter—good and bad—amounted to fifty-three-and-a-half tonnes per acre.

If a thief visited my farm at night and made off with fifty-three-and-a-half tonnes of my best topsoil in the course of a one hour rain that dropped 7.4 cm of precipitation, I would have been horrified, as would any farmer, especially after calculating what it would mean on a field of a hundred acres. The law would have imposed a lifetime sentence for such a crime. The value of soil is recognized much more today than it was even twenty or thirty years ago.

What the Ottawa study demonstrated was the extreme cost of allowing erosion to run wild, which awakened fears of greater and more widespread losses far surpassing those from the experimental plots. Clearly, there are chapters in agricultural history and frontier lore about the neglect of conservation measures that seem to have come from Nature's own book of horror stories. Most of them carry lessons that should not be forgotten.

What should be taken as a solemn warning on every occasion of soil loss from water erosion is that the heaviest losses are almost invisible. Some years ago, a certain quarter section in the Alberta foothills, one that should never have been cultivated, lost one half of its topsoil in a severe summer storm. The loss, however, was carefully assessed and the owner, anxious to protect his remaining inventory of topsoil, immediately ordered a thorough surface cultivation and had the land seeded to grass. Grass can be an apparent miracle worker. In this case, the quarter section is still covered with lush grass and, outwardly, looks very much like the other unbroken quarters nearby.

The lovely Ganaraska River area, a river that runs into Lake Ontario near Port Hope, offers another example. Being hilly and sandy, much of the river region was subject to erosion and was more picturesque than productive, but it had a generous cover of forest trees. As long as the trees remained, the rather fragile natural order enjoyed moderate security. It was fortuitous when citizens near the Ganaraska wanted to know more about the mysteries of the erosion that was drastically changing the local topography. The river had started to create another Grand Canyon, though fortunately it had not yet advanced that far into the job. One of the long-term residents brought forward the compelling theory that the large, eroded coulee on the north side of Port Hope had begun in the nineteenth century with the deep ruts left by wagons hauling heavy loads of logs to accommodate the market for masts and spars needed by the British Navy.

Americans interested in water and erosion tell a similar story of a vast area of agricultural land that was totally destroyed in one of the southern states. The exact location of the disaster has been forgotten but the account remains. It began with a steady drip of rainwater from a barn roof. Doubtless, the soil was of a susceptible kind. The trickle of run-off water gradually created some small rills in the soil. Then the small rills, as they are apt to do, became bigger ones, eventually washing out a road. The soil damage became a farm destroyer and then spread to neighbouring farms. One farm, and then another, was abandoned. Appropriately, the barn from which the trouble had started fell into the now massive trench of its own making. The amount of land ruined due to erosion ultimately totalled twenty-five thousand acres.

Experimental studies directed at the impact of heavy rains on readily erodable soils were followed by academic questions about the widespread tendency of rivers to wash away the best soil. Two of the first soil scientists to answer the call for river investigation were J. J. Milliman and Robert Meade, whose findings were published in the Journal of Geology in 1983. They were probably well aware that all rivers—unless they have glass bottoms—can be expected to carry silt and cause concern for soil conservationists. The size of the river is certainly a factor in determining silt loads but it is not the only one.

In 1995, all the big rivers in north-central Europe were in flood, demonstrating again the distress and the many forms of damage of which flood waters are capable. People and farm animals suffered and drowned by the thousands; bridges were washed out; traffic was paralysed; industry was disrupted and hundreds of thousands of residents evacuated from their homes. Most of the displaced had to sleep on army cots and eat Red Cross food for undetermined periods of time while the water subsided.

Rivers, of course, are versatile and at most times companionable charmers. But with heavy rains or a sudden snow melt, most of them can turn into property destroyers or evil monsters with a special aptitude for stirring up river silt and escorting it to some remote resting place on the floor of an inviting lake or ocean. The people of the Netherlands have spent generations coping with difficult water problems. In a country where more than half the land lies below sea level, shifts in public policy are not made lightly. In light of recent evidence, 1995 will be remembered by them as the worst year since ill-fated 1953, when almost two thousand people lost their lives following a hurricane-induced break in the sea dikes. The Dutch, who say that every experience holds a lesson, are now saying that 1995 was a year for re-assessment, and that rivers present to them a greater permanent danger than lakes or oceans.

Observers of soil erosion will be quick to agree that there is not much that they as individuals can do to arrest the enormous quantities of soil moved by the rivers. All rivers, though, possess a character of their own and better understanding of them could conceivably make for better controls. This interest should not be difficult to instill because many people are strongly captivated by rivers, usually one in particular. Some are drawn to the charm of the small stream, others to the might and mystery of the big river. In any case, the value of a river is too often underestimated by those who place the highest value on the effect it has on the quality of life of an urban community. An attractive river and well-kept riverbed—big or small, wherever it may be—can become a genuine public treasure that is too often taken for granted.

Chapter Seven: The Red River Flood of 1950

During agricultural exploration of the region of North China... I examined the site where the Yellow River broke from its enormous system of inner and outer dikes. As we travelled across the flat plains of Honan, we saw a great flat-topped hill looming up before us. We travelled on over the elevated plain for seven miles to another great dike that stretched from horizon to horizon. We mounted this dike and there before us lay the Yellow River, the Hwang Ho, a great width of brown water flowing quietly that spring morning into a tawny haze in the East.

Here in a channel fully forty or fifty feet [twelve or fifteen metres] above the plain of the great delta lay the river known for thousands of years as China's Sorrow. The giant river had been lifted up off the plain over the entire 400 mile [650 kilometre] course across its delta and had been held in its channel by hand labour of men—without machines or engines, without steel cables or construction timber, and without stone. Millions of Chinese farmers with bare

*The author experiencing the high water levels first hand
after the Red River Flood in 1950.*
(MacEwan Family Archives)

hands and baskets had built here through thousands of years, a stupendous monument to human co-operation and the will to survive. Since the days of Ta-Yu, nearly 4,000 years ago, the battle of floods with this tremendous river have been lost and won time and again.
—W. E. Lowdermilk,
U.S. Department of Agriculture

It is not elongated like the Nile nor ramiform and spreading like the Mississippi. If judged for sheer size beside the Amazon it would suffer like the flea on the back of a dinosaur. Still, the Red River has impressed its own personality on those who live near it. The Red River starts its flow at Lake Traverse on the border between the states of Minnesota and South Dakota, from which point it flows northward to cross the international boundary at Emerson, Manitoba. It then flows through Winnipeg and continues almost straight north to lose itself in Lake Winnipeg, beyond the town of Selkirk. Normally peaceful, the river's worst characteristic has been its urgent desire every few decades to go on a wild flood binge seemingly to prove to itself that, age notwithstanding, it is still capable of doing it.

The Red's first recorded public offence was the devastating flood of 1826, when the Red River colony was in its fifteenth year. The settlers of the region were caught by surprise because they were unaware of the river's previous history of flooding. Its great dangers hidden to them, they built their simple one-room log cabins at the water's edge where they could enjoy the full benefits of easy access to daily water needs and of canoe transportation. (Such were the conveniences of life on the nineteenth-century frontier).

Moreover, the settlers had much to learn about crops and cropping hazards. Not until 1824 did the settlement's fields bear abundantly. Optimism flourished immediately but it was too soon for confidence. The crops of the following year looked promising until, for reasons never thoroughly understood, the settlement was visited at mid-point in the season by a plague of mice who ate almost everything. It became known as the "Year of the Mice." Settlers joked that the rodents had fallen to earth with the rains. The following year, however, was the most destructive of all. It came to be sorrowfully remembered as the "Year of the Great Flood." There had been neither warning nor hint that the flood waters were coming. All of a sudden, the river that had been the settlers' friend, became their worst enemy. People of the Red River Colony saw their cabins and canoes float away and their cultivated fields left too wet for planting. Clutching blankets and a few items of food, they fled on foot to higher ground on Bird's Hill or Stony Mountain.

One courageous soul had the bright idea of moving his bed to the haystack in his stable yard and placing it on top of the hay. The savvy fellow then mounted the stack and prepared to have a sleep. According to the story, he fell asleep but awoke a short time later to find that the river had risen higher and had swept the hay stack into the current with the settler still on board. Apparently, the man in the upper berth was worried but kept calm and plunged into the cold water and managed to swim ashore when the opportunity presented itself.

It was a chilly, wet and disheartening experience but settlers knew that Point Douglas (now a part of Winnipeg) would be no better and were in no hurry to return. Water had performed its "dirty work." What had been so recently a pride-inspiring collection of small homes had become a scene of barren devastation. Thanks to John Pritchard—who also wrote the best account of the violent Seven Oaks Incident in 1816 that had grown out of the rivalry between the Hudson's Bay and Northwest companies— most of the statistics concerning 1826 have survived to the present time. It is known that the flood level rose over two-and-a-half metres on May second and continued to rise until the twenty-first of that month. The small log homes didn't survive for very long in the onslaught of water. Francis Heron, an employee of the Hudson's Bay Company, witnessed forty-seven of the log buildings float away in the space of half an hour, some of them still intact, some falling apart, leaving hardly a house in the settlement still standing.

By the end of May, when the floods were showing signs of subsiding, Pritchard saw depressed settlers trudging back to their plots of land, but it was impossible to plant anything until the middle of June. A few utterly demoralized settlers quit the settlement altogether. Others, like Pritchard, were back on the farm after an enforced absence of twelve weeks, wondering what to do with the year's crop and where to start over.

In the next 124 years, the Red River kicked up a few floods—1852, 1882, 1887 and 1948—but nothing rivalling the amount of water seen in 1826. Some observers said the Red River had repented and hoped that it had outgrown its irascible ways. They could never have foreseen that the flood of 1950 would shatter all previous records.

In April and May of 1950, weather favoured flooding. The autumn rains had been well above normal and soil moisture was extremely high. To make matters worse, the winter snowfall had been heavier than usual and the spring thaws were late, as if inviting more precipitation before the winter snow had disappeared.

On the first of April, Winnipeg's City Engineer, W. D. Hurst, read the ominous meteorological signs and sounded a public flood-warning. He set about ensuring that the river dikes were in good repair and essential new ones were being constructed. The first week in May looked more frightening than ever. From the air, the southern Manitoba towns of Emerson and Morris looked like two lighthouse islands in Canada's most recent Great Lake—a body of water a hundred kilometres wide in places and up to three metres deep. An engineer on the job quipped that the ancient Lake Agassiz, which had once covered much of southern Manitoba, had produced an offspring.

Traffic in parts of Winnipeg came to a halt as river water spilled over the banks. On May 6, Premier Douglas Campbell asked a military unit to take emergency control after the area had been officially declared a national disaster. Within hours, eight hundred members of the Princess Patricia's Canadian Light Infantry from Calgary flew to Winnipeg under the command of Brigadier R.E.A. Morton and entered at once into every aspect of the emergency for the next three weeks.

One hundred thousand Winnipegers fled the city to accept the comforts and security offered by friends and relatives in other parts of Canada and beyond. It was declared to be the largest mass exodus in Canadian history. Another hundred thousand became volunteer workers under the most humble of circumstances: caring for the sick, making meals for all comers, finding beds and shelters for the needy or filling sandbags for the innumerable dikes. It was later declared one of the finest displays of volunteerism ever witnessed by Canadians. The task that fell to this author, then living on Somerset Avenue in Fort Garry and teaching at the University of Manitoba, was to be in service as the man on sewer gang duty through the midnight hours. My responsibility was to keep a municipal International 15-30 farm tractor, connected to a pump, running non-stop to ensure against sewage backups in Fort Garry homes.

The Red River flood water crested on May thirteenth but the return to normal levels was slow. The army did not see fit to relinquish complete authority for another two weeks. Citizens were immediately more cheerful. A home owner replaced the "For Sale" sign on his front lawn with one that read "I paid $17,000 for this house. Will sell it for $17." As property owners tallied their losses it was found that small communities had suffered the most. The town of Morris, with 368 homes and fifty-one places of business, had seen forty-one of those homes float away. Only four buildings in town did not have water covering their floors. Altogether, more than ten thousand homes had been involved in the fight against flood water and governments were already promising financial assistance for repairs and reconstruction.

By the date for the military withdrawal on the last day of May, the river level had dropped one and a half metres from the record flood-crest of nine metres on May ninteenth. The river level, however, was still two metres above flood stage. On that same date, Manitoba's Premier Campbell announced the appointment of a Flood Relief Review Board consisting of three Manitoba residents: C. E. Joslyn of Winnipeg, Walter Forrester, former Mayor of Emerson, and this author, then Dean of Agriculture at the University of Manitoba. Members of the board would begin sittings at once and all citizens who had suffered property damage in any form could apply to be heard and have their damages assessed.

Farmers with livestock had added flood problems but ingenuity generally paid off. One way or another, nearly all the animals had been brought to the safety of dry ground. At St. Adolphe, twenty-six cattle owned by six farmers were held on a river scow for two weeks until they were evacuated by a barge to the only dry spot left in the district. Another farmer jacked up a grain storage bin and kept six cattle and two horses in it. On the University of Manitoba farm south of Winnipeg, the dairy cattle and pigs were housed for the flood's duration in stockcars on a railway spur line. Feed was delivered to them by rowboat. The sheep flock, on the other hand, survived the flood in the hayloft of the horse barn and none of them suffered.

From the point of view of erosion, it is difficult to assess accurately the effect the flood had on farm land. It takes moving water and loose soil to produce erosion so it is doubtful whether the flood water that became stilled on Manitoba and Minnesota fields in 1950 actually generated a great deal of erosion. Nevertheless, the soil owner should guard against becoming overly trusting in matters of soil and water. Although the erosion along the Red in 1950 was not intense, it affected a very large area of farmland and the loss was probably much greater than was then realized.

It is difficult to find net benefits from a big flood but the blessing in disguise in this instance was the decision by the government of Manitoba to build the costly forty-seven-kilometre-long Red River Floodway. Designed to divert a substantial part of any floodwater around the city of Winnipeg, the Floodway was tested again and again by small to medium-sized floods, with impressive results. The question remained, though, as to how the big ditch would cope with a massive flood like that of 1950 or an even larger one.

The flood in the spring of 1997 was to put the Floodway to the ultimate test and permanently silence the sceptics. The small Red River town of St. Agathe was one of the first to report flood trouble in 1997. The scope of the disaster became immediately apparent. Manitobans realized at once their need for help from the Armed Forces; they gladly and immediately accepted the assistance of seven thousand personnel and heavy vehicles from the Canadian Armed Forces. The billowing waves of the Red brought the flood level higher by the minute until the crest was announced on May second. By that time, flood relief programs were already in operation and reporting generous responses. Nobody drew benefits; nobody expected them. The Canadian Red Cross, by the fourth week of May, having adopted the slogan "Ten Million Reasons to Care," could report ten million dollars in the fund and more coming in at an accelerated rate.

Thanks in large part to the work of the Canadian Army, most of the twenty-eight thousand people who were forced from their flooded homes were back or on their way back by the end of May. They were convinced of one point: without the Floodway, their disaster would have been greater and much more costly.

PART IV. MANAGING WATER
Chapter Eight: Dams, Dugouts and George Spence

The new frontier in agriculture is the conservation of water resources. Wherever water can be used for irrigation, let's have eight families living on a quarter section instead of one family living on four sections of land. It isn't possible to preserve soil fertility in many areas by the crop-and-summer fallow system, common in dry land farming. But irrigation can be made not only to preserve but increase fertility.

I believe in the theory that it is nothing short of a crime to allow water to run across the dry land down to the ocean without making an effort to conserve it and use it to augment the scanty supply Nature allows us.

This is the thing we've got to remember: We can't forever go on writing cheques against Nature's bank account without thought of depletion. We must devise methods that return in some measure what we are taking out of the soil. The use of soil-building crops and improved cultural methods are a step in the

Dr. George Spence, Irrigation pioneer.
(Glenbow Museum Archives, NA-242-1)

right direction. And we'll need more irrigation
water.

—George Spence, 1947

The small Orkney Islands of Scotland have made their principal contribution to world agriculture by meeting most of the food needs of their twenty-four thousand island residents. The economy of the seventy-five islands rests largely on fishing, especially for brown and sea trout. Some writers seem to go out of their way to lament that, in the distribution of natural resources, the Orkney Islands received less than their fair share. They cite the absence of rivers, the dearth of mineable minerals, the paucity of merchandisable forests and the shortage of spectacular natural scenery of the type to enrapture tourists. But just as frequently, some of the rich gifts of Nature have been overlooked. For example, the Orkneys have a pleasant range of climatic conditions and a generous average precipitation of close to seventy-six centimetres per year.

What is often taken for granted is the islands' wealth of human resources, the qualities of character that make up for the starkness of the landscape. The stout spirit and unfailing resourcefulness of the Orkney men were favoured by the Hudson's Bay Company during the days of the fur trade. Recruitment officials sought out Orkney Islanders specifically in their bid to recruit the most reliable and versatile workers for contract service in the rugged conditions of Rupert's Land.

George Spence carried that spirit. He was invited to sign a Hudson's Bay contract but he wanted to test the employment "waters" in other areas first, including an apprenticeship course in electrical engineering at the University of Edinburgh. The course was of interest to him but he found it was too far removed from his first loves: the soil, trees, animals and farming. The Edinburgh experience prompted the tall, lean and athletic George Spence to consider his own vocational future more seriously. It would have been easy to settle back into the dual career of farmer and fisherman, but there was always the consolation that he could return to it later.

Spence came to the Canadian Northwest and saw the prairies in one of their drier spells. But that was fine; he was eager to see everything. After travelling to the Yukon he quickly divined that the miners who came during the Klondike Gold Rush of 1898 didn't leave much for the latecomers. So with luck on his side, he obtained a paying job on a local land survey and remained in the Yukon for almost three years. He had not intended to stay that long, but what else could he do? He was caught up by the "spell of the Yukon," and had good fortune in reworking some gravel bars that had been abandoned prematurely by earlier miners. It was still very much in his thoughts to make a return crossing of the Canadian prairies, though he wasn't in a hurry. He wanted to find answers to questions he had about the fertility of the land and verify for himself the negative assessment of Captain John Palliser, the influential explorer who had written off the agricultural potential of the southern prairies following his fact-finding trip from 1857 to 1860.

When news of the creation of the two new provinces of
Saskatchewan and Alberta reached George Spence, he was
travelling somewhere southwest of Moose Jaw with the help of
a borrowed horse and saddle, a roll of blankets and a well
stocked canvas bag of food supplies. The horse was tethered
amid good grazing at night, and also at any time during the day
when Spence wished to pause and make notes about soil,
scenery, trees and water resources.

What had been called the "spell of the Yukon" was becoming for Spence in 1912 the "spell of the Prairies." His choice of
Saskatchewan homestead land was a quarter section on the US
border almost straight south of Swift Current. As he saw it, the
countryside looked lush and green, unusually so because of the
exceptionally heavy rains in that year. At Calgary, where the
year's precipitation bore some similarity to that of the southern
prairies, fifty-three centimetres had fallen, the highest since
1902, which misled many aspiring landowners.

After paying the ten dollar filing fee with his homestead
application, Spence knew that to qualify for a clear title to the
land at the end of three years he was required to have a hab-
itable house in place, although anything from a shack to a
mansion would serve the purpose. He would also be required
to break and cultivate a specified amount of land—often just
ten acres—and be in residence on the land for at least six
months out of each year. A homesteader was not required to
plant crops but anyone who knew George Spence would
expect him to challenge the region's reputation for drought
and unsuitability for trees.

One of his first tasks as a homesteader was to apply to the

government tree nursery at Indian Head for 1,500 tree seedlings. In due course he was notified that, in the absence of a railway to the remote homestead district, the shipment of seedlings would be delivered to Neville, not far from Swift Current and about a hundred kilometres north of his homestead. Transportation was not provided from the rail-line, so how was he going to bring the trees to his land? Spence didn't seem worried about the problem. He walked the ninety-seven kilometres to Neville and packed the seedlings in a parcel that was safe for travelling. He matter-of-factly placed the bulky and heavy package on his back and strode the long trail back home. One week after Spence had taken possession of the seedlings, they were in the ground and he was praying for rain. It was indeed a treeless part of the Palliser Triangle, but Spence's prayers were answered. The rains came, and his homestead, dubbed the Orkney Farm, became an agricultural showpiece.

Spence was a scholarly fellow by nature and soon realized that to be successful in the fight against drought, he should be drawing on the experience of water-wise people who had visited the prairies before him. He acquainted himself with the writings of Captain John Palliser, Henry Youle Hind, Sandford Fleming and, most of all, William Pearce, whom Spence said was "nothing short of a genius" in laying the groundwork for the development of water resources in the West.

By 1917, Spence could no longer resist politics as a means of furthering his evolving ideas about water. He was elected to represent his homestead region in the Saskatchewan Legislature and, over the next twenty years, was a successful provincial and federal candidate on seven occasions. His principal mission in both levels of government never stopped being the advancement of water conservation and management.

On his own dry land, he had seen some good crop years and some dismal failures. He had mournful memories of the 1930s. Yet, significantly, he was still on his land at the end of the decade. He wanted to be honest about the gloom, and wrote about what it was like to live through it in his 1967 book *Survival of a Vision*:

> *It would be almost impossible to exaggerate the terrible conditions brought about by the unprecedented drought of the "black thirties." This drought cycle began in 1929 after a record-breaking crop produced over the greater part of the plains area in the previous year. It continued with varying intensity across a vast area of the prairie provinces for eight distressing years, 1929-37. Only those who lived through the privations wrought by it could be expected to have a proper conception of the grim conditions of that time. The awful reality of the situation was evidenced in grain fields laid waste, pastures smothered beneath layers of dry dust as "black blizzards" lashed across the land, lifting clouds of topsoil into the air, darkening the noon day sun, and turning the whole landscape into a sea of bouncing tumbleweed to pile against fences, block roadways and fill farm shelterbelts with great drifts of blow dirt so flour-fine as to sift*

*through every crack and cranny of the dwelling,
settling on floors and furnishings, contaminat-
ing food and distracting the occupants almost
beyond human endurance.*

Most prairie observers were ready to accept the view that
the 1930s were the driest years in memory, but Spence pointed
to the years from 1917 to 1921 as having been drier still.
Calgary records agreed, showing total precipitation of only
twenty-three centimetres in 1918, a figure lower than the driest
single year recorded at the same station in the 1930s. In the
years of average or better-than-average rainfall, the western
prairies had furnished enough wheat to make Canada a world
leader in exports. Buoyed by optimism, farm leaders issued a
proposal that the 1932 World's Grain Show be brought to
Regina. It was to fulfil a dream long held by the region, but
drought and economic gloom forced the Canadian committee
to seek permission to postpone the prestigious event for a year.
The show was finally staged in 1933 under heart-breakingly
bleak conditions.

Though not expecting the government to change the
weather, people in Western Canada began calling on it to do
something about the deepening crisis. At about the midpoint
of the Depression, both Prime Minister R. B. Bennett and
Robert Weir, Bennett's Minister of Agriculture—who had
been a farmer himself at Weldon, Saskatchewan—made their
own fact-finding tours. They brought with them the promise
of a major government aid programme to rescue the seriously
depressed agricultural industry. Most people did not know

what to expect, but reasoned that anything would be better than drifting soil, parched fields, starving livestock and abandoned farms.

The eagerly-awaited Prairie Farm Rehabilitation Act cleared Parliament with uncharacteristic speed and received Royal Assent on April 17, 1935. Known almost invariably as the PFRA, the Act was born with a built-in provision for the public funds needed for the first year of operations. It stated that "The sum of seven hundred and fifty thousand dollars shall be appropriated and paid out of the Consolidated Revenue of Canada during the fiscal year, 1935-36, and for each fiscal year for a further period of four years a sum not exceeding one million dollars per annum as may be necessary to continue and extend the work undertaken under this Act." An impatient and demoralized public sought instant, visible evidence of progress. Some early proof came with the relatively heavy programme of urgently needed farm reservoirs created by dugouts and small dams.

George Spence, who became the first Director of the PFRA Administration and held the office for nine years, was particularly pleased to report evidence of the popularity of small water developments. He noted that in the first year of the PFRA, 645 of the small water projects were completed. By the end of 1965 the number of projects completed under the Act totalled 94,482. The infant PFRA did much to improve its image across the entire West over the decades, especially when it was able to take credit for 110,000 new farm dugouts for water that might have been lost to runoff.

Everybody knew that the setting up of community pastures

on land that could not sustain conventional farming would be like a dream come true for many farmers. Even before the PFRA was a confirmed statute, Spence was sitting on a national commitee with the simple purpose of winning government interest in community pastures on poor land. In the course of this committee's work, Spence was said to have asked a farmer from Val Marie, Saskatchewan for his recommendations regarding community pastures. Not recognizing Spence, the man told him to "talk to George Spence who farms at Orkney. Make sure you listen carefully, and be damned sure you close Spence's gate when you're leaving." The PFRA Administration began assembling and operating community pastures in 1937. By the time of its fiftieth anniversary it had eighty-eight community pastures across the West, furnishing grazing for 230,000 head of livestock.

The PFRA was engaged in other services as well. The large federal tree distribution programme with its huge tree nursery at Indian Head was transferred to the PFRA in 1963 and continued to process ten thousand applications for prairie plantings per year. In 1985 it was reported that more than 450 million tree seedlings had been transplanted from the federal nurseries since the service had begun eighty-three years earlier—enough young trees to furnish a shelter belt around the world.

One of Spence's most high profile undertakings as the director of the PFRA was to agitate for the building of a large dam and water reservoir on the South Saskatchewan River. The idea for the dam was a natural extension of the PFRA's mandate to bring about a more diversified agricultural system in low rainfall areas. The process of studying, approving and

building the dam was eventually to take on monumental proportions, political tribulations notwithstanding. Everything
about the project was big: its dimensions, its cost and even its
distinction of bringing together three of Canada's most famous
politicians from three different political parties at the federal
and provincial levels—the Liberal Minister of Agriculture
James G. Gardiner (who held that post for a record period,
1935-57), the Conservative leader and later Prime Minister
John G. Diefenbaker, and the premier of Saskatchewan,
Thomas C. Douglas, of the CCF.

The creation of a dam and reservoir somewhere along the
South Saskatchewan River was not a new idea; it could be
traced back to the observations Henry Youle Hind made following his 1858 geological expedition to the area. But serious
consideration of the idea had been held back by issues of feasibility and cost. In 1943, after Spence met with Gardiner and
convinced him of the necessity of the project, he then became
a long-time champion and driving force of the plan.

The proposed dam would permit better use of the South
Saskatchewan River water for irrigation of an estimated
455,000 acres of land in Central Saskatchewan. It was also to
meet the domestic water needs of the cities of Moose Jaw and
Regina, as well as aid in flood control, produce hydroelec-
tricity, and create a recreational lake. There would be need
for two dams, a big one to impound and hold the main
reserve, and a smaller one to prevent the water in the principal reservoir from escaping into the Qu'Appelle Valley.

Amid fears and controversy, an official independent
appraisal of the project was launched. On August 24, 1951, an

Order In Council appointed commissioners to conduct an enquiry into the project to assess its cost effectiveness. The final report was less than enthusiastic: "The Commission finds that at present the economic returns to the Canadian people on the investment on the proposed South Saskatchewan River Project are not commensurate with the cost involved; though the Project would yield social returns which, while they cannot be measured for the purposes of this report, would be of great value to the region in which it is situated." The report could have been expected to produce some embarrassment and probably did, but politicians are not easily embarrassed, and as far as is known, nobody suffered from it.

After the tabling of the report, Gardiner and Spence (now serving on the International Joint Commission, which dealt with issues growing out of the rivers and lakes shared by the United States and Canada) were having difficulty convincing Prime Minister Louis St. Laurent of the viability of the project. As Conservative Opposition Leader, Diefenbaker campaigned in the 1957 election on a platform that included the promise to build the South Saskatchewan Dam. When his party ultimately formed the next government, work on the project began in earnest.

According to the terms of the agreement struck with the federal government, the Province of Saskatchewan became responsible for the construction and cost of the irrigation works required for up to 520,000 acres along the South Saskatchewan River between Elbow and Saskatoon, and in the Qu'Appelle Valley as far as the Manitoba border. Work on the South Saskatchewan Dam project began in 1958 and continued with no more than normal delays. The town of Elbow began to look like a metropolis as construction advanced. Farmers with deep reservations about the practicality of irrigation in the region came to watch in silence, wondering how the new and soaring debts were to be paid—a hundred million dollars here, a hundred million dollars there. The dam was completed in 1967 and named after Gardiner, while the reservoir that it formed, with its four billion cubic metres of storage capacity, was named Lake Diefenbaker.

If there was a moral to be noted, it was that irrigation water can produce what seem to be miracles, and that men and women in public life should understand that it is possible to pay too much, even for miracles. For his part, George Spence continued to deal with water issues on the International Joint Commission and to observe from a distance the fruitful unfolding of the innumerable agricultural projects he had overseen on the prairies.

Construction of the Bassano Dam on the Bow River, Alberta c. 1914.
(Glenbow Museum Archives, NA-4389-105)

Chapter Nine: Irrigating Southern Alberta

As far as the world's food is concerned, all people must learn together to make proper use of the earth on which we live. Hovering even now over our shoulders is a spectre as sinister as the atomic bomb because it could de-populate the earth and destroy our cities. This creeping terror is the wastage of the world's natural resources and particularly the exploitation of the soil. What will it profit us to achieve the H bomb and survive that tragedy, or triumph if the generations that succeed us must starve in a world because of our misuse, grown barren as the mountains of the moon. —Dwight Eisenhower, 1950

Throughout the ages, irrigation has become a "strong right arm" of world agriculture. These two interlocking practices were born at about the same point in ancient history and in the same general areas—close to the Euphrates and Tigris Rivers in Mesopotamia, and along the Egyptian Nile. It was dry, desert country that resisted all cropping unless moisture was brought to it by artificial means.

Irrigation came to the eastern part of the North American continent long before it was adopted in more arid western regions, for obvious reasons. The middle-eastern region was the first to be settled and, having heavier average rainfall, settlers had less need for irrigation. Further west, the single biggest influence was Captain John Palliser, the red-haired Irish bachelor and engineer who came as a servant of the Imperial British Government to report on the future of Britain's Rupert's Land. Palliser had been in the region before on a prolonged buffalo hunt. In the course of his more formal duties, he saw the Western Canadian prairies as an "extension of the Great American desert," and judged it to be of doubtful value for agriculture and settlement. It was too dry, he proclaimed, to justify high hopes for anything more than the grazing of buffalo or cattle. The region might have excited dreams of irrigation, but where could the water be obtained in sufficient amounts?

Human imagination, however, rarely fails to find a way around a problem. When a housewife carried a bucket of pond water from a nearby slough to refresh the garden tomatoes growing in her boxes, she may have been one of the first irrigators in Western Canada. The first person to apply irrigation on a broad scale, however, was another Irishman, John Glenn. Initially drawn to British Columbia by the Caribou Gold Rush of the early 1860s, Glenn then trekked eastward across the Rockies to Fort Edmonton where he paused to pan for gold in the North Saskatchewan River gravel. In 1874, he decided to move south and squatted on a piece of land beside Fish Creek, a tributary of the Bow River not far from the shadow of the

Rockies. This was a year before the Mounted Police arrived to build Fort Calgary beside the Bow. Glenn tapped Fish Creek and ditched the water eastward to irrigate between ten and twenty acres of attractive bottom land immediately below today's Lacombe Home. Glenn's endeavours single him out as the first to practice irrigation in Western Canada, and perhaps the entire country.

Others, like John Quirk, a pioneer cattleman who settled along Sheep Creek, followed Glenn's example but did not gain much public notice. It took a spokesman and leader like William Pearce to make the newcomers conscious of what they might achieve with irrigation water. Pearce, an Ontario-raised boy, came to the prairies in 1874—the same year as the Mounted Police came to Fort Macleod. He came as a servant of the Dominion Department of the Interior and remained to become a leader in survey organization, mining and irrigation. His almost religious zeal for making the best use of water resources was instrumental in bringing irrigation to the dry parts of the West, particularly the area that became southern Alberta. Pearce's dream was irrigation for central Alberta and south-central Saskatchewan with water from the North Saskatchewan, Red Deer and South Saskatchewan Rivers. It was a scheme that might have changed the agriculture of much of the prairie country, and one that certainly gripped Pearce until his death in 1930.

Pearce was an engineer by training, a conservationist by instinct, and a tree planter and irrigationist by desire. As Superintendent of Lands and Mines for the Territories, he settled in Calgary in 1882 and proceeded to build a massive stone house that was long regarded as Calgary's finest. At the same time, he planted trees and began turning his thoughts to large-scale irrigation. He was also the first to sound warnings that the day would come when the demand for irrigation water would exceed the supply in settled parts of the country.

Pearce's growing interest in irrigation drew him to Utah where the Mormons had already made notable progress employing various methods. On his return, he proposed the boldest scheme for irrigation that had ever been advanced in Canada. It would solve the Canadian Pacific Railway's problems in obtaining water for its steam engines on the rails and, more importantly, attract settlers. Although fascinated, both the federal government and railway authorities disliked the idea of admitting to the public that the vast lands they were keen to settle were so dry that they required irrigation. The earliest proposals based on the Pearce Plan were turned down. The stubborn and energetic Pearce was undaunted and, in 1894, he took water from the Elbow River near Bragg Creek and conducted it to his east Calgary home site to demonstrate the benefits irrigation could have for growing grain, supporting grazing and producing vegetable crops.

The Canadian Pacific Railway and the Canadian government could not ignore the irrefutable proof that irrigation was both possible and highly beneficial. William Pearce was making headway. He then proposed that the CPR construct a dam on the Bow River near Bassano, Alberta, one that would provide water for their steam locomotives, furnish drinking water for the needs of railroad labourers and meet the needs of incoming settlers and ranchers. The railroad company was finally convinced. In 1910, the Bassano dam was started at the town that later proudly labelled itself "The Best Town By A Dam Site" and completed four years later.

The grand dream became the cornerstone of the William Pearce Plan, which called for a vast irrigation system capable of watering a large area between the North and South Saskatchewan Rivers. Pearce began advocating such a plan in 1898 and did not stop trying to rally support for it until his death in 1930. By means of a series of dams, he believed he could divert the North Saskatchewan River to points above Rocky Mountain House, then conduct the water to the Clearwater and Red Deer Rivers for use as reservoirs. Pearce was sure he would see storage for enough water to irrigate a million acres of the dry Saskatchewan prairies and half a million acres in Alberta. His bold plans have never been acted upon but some contemporary engineers say they are still feasible, and a modified version of the project may in time bear fruit.

Nevertheless, Pearce's ideas have had a large impact on Western Canadian water policy and development. The multi-million dollar project (mentioned in the previous chapter) to build the Gardiner Dam, beginning in the late 1950s, drew heavily on Pearce's blueprints for developing the South Saskatchewan River. As well, the federal government's 1894 "North-West Irrigation Act," which was significantly shaped by Pearce, continues to influence all Western Canadian water policies, aside from those concerning groundwater. The Act has meant that the diversion or impounding of water from any stream is forbidden except by licence.

For its part, the Canadian Pacific Railway Company

implemented many of Pearce's ideas and became one of the biggest irrigation developers on the continent. Under the terms of the CPR's contract with the Dominion Government in 1881, the rail company was given all the odd-numbered sections within thirty-nine kilometres of both sides of the company's mainline, thereby giving it a fundamental interest in land settlement as well as irrigation. A short time later, Sir William Van Horne, scarcely less enthusiastic about irrigation than Pearce himself, became president of the railroad and solidified the company's new direction.

By an act of Parliament in 1894, the CPR was allowed to take its development of land between Medicine Hat and Crowfoot, Alberta in two unbroken blocks in order to facilitate the Pearce and Van Horne designs for irrigation. The water for the western block of about three million acres would come from the Bow River not far from Calgary. That project of record size was started in 1904 and completed seven years later. Work on the eastern CPR block was undertaken next, and halted when the Bassano Dam raised the water level of the Bow River. Canals were ready for water in the spring of 1914. Now the CPR, combining experience in irrigation and shrewd business management, became the biggest irrigator on the continent. It could boast an integrated operation that included, in addition to transportation, land sales, irrigation, oil and gas development, mining, hotels, and promotion on many fronts.

Irrigation received its next big boost from the Southern Alberta Land Company, backed by English money. Headed by J.D. McGregor, one of Manitoba's most successful cattlemen, the company prepared to sell irrigated land as "ready-made" family farms in a secured area near Medicine Hat. Much of the land to be irrigated had been previously held by McGregor as a grazing lease. The company purchased the land from the federal Department of the Interior at a nominal price on the assurance that a certain percentage of it would be irrigated for the settlers, most of whom were expected to come from England. The cost of irrigation and development was expected to exceed fifteen million dollars. Water was to be taken from the Bow River at a point near Gleichen—about sixty miles east of Calgary—and conducted east and south through Snake Valley. Lake McGregor was the artificial lake and reservoir that would be created at the south end of the valley.

Canadian Wheatlands was organized in England in 1911 as an offshoot of the Southern Alberta Land Company. An option to purchase was taken on 64,000 acres of the parent company's land. Two-thirds of the land covered by the option were to be ready to receive irrigation water no later than 1914. Twelve thousand acres of the land were broken in 1911, and thirteen thousand more in the next year, but the plans started to unravel and soon fell apart completely. Even now, more than eighty years later, travellers between Vauxhall and Medicine Hat can see long stretches of irrigation ditches that have never been used.

There were many other disappointments, but some of the big irrigation companies met with success. The first one to receive a Dominion charter, the Galt Ranching Company, founded by the Galt family of Lethbridge, was irrigating by 1897. Then there was the High River and Sheep Creek

Irrigation Company and the Alberta Irrigation Company, both moderately successful. The St. Mary and Milk River Development, commanding widespread attention, was started in 1947 and completed in 1951. Especially noteworthy was the Lethbridge Northern, a well-known community co-operative that began by taking water from the Oldman River. With good and sound leadership, it served its purpose well.

Nor were the professional rainmakers who claimed to have found the secret of producing rain on demand denied a place in the development of the region. Early in 1921, for example, an American by the name of Charles Hatfield agreed to bring his chemicals and rainmaking techniques to Medicine Hat for a fee. He signed a contract with the United Agricultural Association and the area in which he would increase rainfall was marked out with a three-kilometre radius on a map. It was agreed that he would take credit for half of the rain that fell between May 1 and August 1 and collect up to a maximum of $8,000 for a rainfall of a hundred millimetres beyond the arranged minimum. The clever fellow set up his tower from which he would release mysterious chemicals and vapours beside a small lake not far from Medicine Hat. The public was thankful for the entertainment, unprecedented as it was. Farmers from miles around drove to "the Hat" to buy raincoats and rubber boots.

A few days after Hatfield's equipment was installed and the miracle fumes were uncorked, rain began to fall. It continued to fall lightly for several days until a few farmers who needed fair weather for good haying came to town to find Hatfield and beg him to "shut it off." If publicity was what

Hatfield wanted he was getting it in abundance. Unfortunately for his business and reputation as a rainmaker, other districts across southern Alberta were also getting his "miraculous" rain. The neighbouring districts beyond the Hatfield contract radius were receiving more rain than "the Hat," and Hatfield's sceptics multiplied. The great salesman, however, collected the payments to which he said he was entitled and offered to return the next year. He did not return, and many people thought he was wise not to push his luck.

In 1926, five years after the Hatfield experiment, the government of Alberta appointed a commission to make a thorough study of one of its most troublesome areas: Tilley East, situated near the apex of the Palliser Triangle. Its main problem was shortage of moisture, just as Palliser might have foretold. The area did not have a reserve of nearby water upon which to draw for irrigation. The commission served its purpose well. Instead of producing miracles, it brought together some useful information about land irrigation for incorporation in legislation for the Special Areas Act.

As governments continued to search for remedial measures for dealing with drought areas, the Special Areas Act was seen as a forerunner to the federal government's benchmark Prairie Farm Rehabilitation Act passed in the middle of the drought and depression-plagued 1930s. The Great Depression—those memorable and ugly times that North Americans will never forget—was no laughing matter, but there were those cheerful souls whose unfailing sense of humour refused to yield. Happily, some of their humorous anecdotes involving water shortages have survived. According to one report, the lack of water was so serious at Maple Creek, Saskatchewan that persons unable to obtain the customary water for baptisms were obliged to use dry soil. One farmer said everything was so dry at his place that he had to soak the family sow in the spring for two days before she could hold swill. Another resident of the area, witnessing dust blizzards day after day, reported seeing a gopher digging a shelter for himself in a cloud of dust three metres off the ground.

Some settlers abandoned their farms and departed for parts unknown. Others refused to leave. The story goes that during this period an urban traveller looking for water to relieve his overheated radiator called at two farms. He soon realized it was not his lucky day. At the first place there was no one home, just an explanatory poem tacked to the door:

It's fifty miles to water,
A hundred miles to wood.
To hell with sunny Alberta,
We've left it for good.

The second farmhouse was also empty and, strangely enough, it too had a note on the door:

It's fifty miles to water,
One hundred miles to wood.
To hell with California,
We're staying here for good.
P.S. Visitors make yourselves at home. We've gone fishing.

It is clear that the gigantic Canadian Pacific Railway irrigation projects in Western Canada were a boon to agriculture, especially in Alberta. However, as is generally the case with monopolistic arrangements, friction developed between producer and consumer, the latter in this case being the farmers who were beholden to the railway company for the use of their irrigated water. In short, they were increasingly sure that they were paying too much for the water. "We are the water users who must pay the bills," the farmers complained, "and we should be the ones to set the rate of payment." For its part, the CPR was equally convinced of the righteousness of its cause. The bitter debate that followed constitutes one of the most interesting chapters in Western Canadian farm history. The disagreement was not to be resolved easily. The settlers contended that fifty dollars an acre for land provided with irrigation water was too high and that the CPR hadn't proved its claim that high operating costs justified the rates being levied. Furthermore, they argued that the CPR had misled them at the time of purchase by making their farms look like bargains.

The Depression following World War One aggravated the bickering. The CPR had hinted, perhaps facetiously, that if the water users believed they could do a better job, then they should buy all the land and try it. Although railway officials were aware of statements suggesting that water users were considering a takeover, the CPR deemed the claim unrealistic boasting. In the meantime, there were changes taking place in farm leadership circles, one of the most notable being the election of farmer Carl Anderson to the presidency of the Scandia United Farmers of Alberta. Under Anderson's direction, the matter of a farmer-takeover of the CPR's Eastern Irrigation

District (EID) came into clearer focus. A committee was formed under Anderson with a mandate to approach the CPR on the subject of a possible takeover.

The idea of a takeover of those assets that the CPR was having difficulty maintaining was probably received with some uncertainty in railway circles. Yet the fact that the CPR did not immediately respond either positively or negatively served to strengthen the commitment of the amateur businessmen. The farmers' committee had already resolved not to be rushed by the CPR in the event of any negotiations actually taking place. It continued to wait until the results of two votes taken by all water users clearly indicated they were in favour of an irrigation district and supported timely discussions with the officers of the CPR. The next step was to learn the exact price and the amount of cash the CPR could be expected to pay the farmer-led group for assuming responsibility for the EID's extensive operations.

With Carl Anderson as spokesman, a water user's committee told the Montréal men that their original offer of $100,000 would not even pay for the farmers' chewing tobacco debts. They needed $400,000. A smiling Anderson politely refused the CPR's counter-offer and suggested the meeting be adjourned so they could develop a more realistic proposal. An evening meeting was approved at which the Montréalers raised their cash offer to $200,000. Anderson again shook his head and asked for a short recess. The recess was welcomed. Anderson's trio huddled quickly, expecting to be asked by Anderson, "to hold out" for the proposed $400,000. One committee member worried that being overly intransigent might mean the collapse of the entire negotiations and indicated his willingness to accept the CPR's latest offer of $200,000. Anderson admitted that the group might have to compromise slightly but not to the point of giving away too much. Anderson suggested they stand firm on the $400,000, but also request more time in the event of a refusal.

The joint meeting was reconvened. Although the committee re-stated its original price, a suggestion was added to the effect that if the CPR revised its offer the farmers might be prepared to compromise on their end. "Make us an offer," said Anderson, "and see what happens." The CPR countered with a final offer of $300,000 which was duly accepted.

It was 1935, mid-point in the Great Depression. The CPR was about to turn over a large chunk of its irrigation empire, along with titles to facilities of great value and a substantial sum of money to cover existing debts. The unprecedented deal was incorporated into Chapter 101 of the Revised Statutes of Alberta and further dignified by a special act of the legislature. With the creation of the first board of trustees for the Eastern Irrigation District, a dream became a reality.

Looking back at that period in history, one can honestly ponder the issue, not of the viability of irrigation in agricultural programs, but rather their extent and the ultimate source of funding for them. Should government funding of irrigation projects be in the nature of gifts or loans to water users? Should the government that subsidizes prairie irrigation be expected to do any less for land drainage in the North where the problem of too much water in the soil is equally important? Should government funding of irrigation projects take into account the serious problem of salt build-up in irrigated soil?

Dr. Arleigh Laycock, professor of geography at the University of Alberta, has long argued against large-scale irrigation projects, often in the face of strident criticism. "Huge irrigation projects are folly," he has said. "Modest development at modest cost, close involvement of the people of the region, and careful use of resources, is probably preferable to massive and costly development that a region or province cannot afford."

Whatever the future of irrigation in Alberta there have been individuals in the past who have risen to the challenge of changing conditions and they will certainly do so in the future.

Chapter Ten: Dutch Influence On Alberta

I have but one lamp by which my feet are guided and that is the lamp of experience. I know of no way of judging the future but by the past.

—Patrick Henry

The practical people of the Netherlands were known to wish many times that they had more land and less surplus water. If only they could obtain good land and pay for it with salty water, they would soon be as land-rich as Texans. The Dutch conflict between the salty seawater, seemingly impossible to keep out, and the comparatively salt-free rivers might, for Canadians, bring to mind similar conflicts between the excellent drinking water found in some prairie wells and the dangerously high levels of alkali salts found in others.

The people of what is now the Netherlands have struggled for centuries with the fluctuating levels of the Zuiderzee (also know as the North Sea) which forms a long inlet into the centre of the country's landmass. As early as 1000 AD people began constructing dikes and high mounds in order to temper these effects and over the following centuries developed

*A windmill at Bruderheim, Alberta. This mill was
moved to Heritage Park in Calgary in 1983.*
(Glenbow Museum Archives, NA-290-1)

"empoldering," or land reclamation, techniques. By the seventeenth century these techniques were so advanced that authorities proposed the building of a seawall that would cut off the Zuiderzee from the inland areas and create a more stable environment for the land that had been reclaimed.

It was not until after the disastrous floods of 1916, however, that these ambitious plans were revived by the great engineer-statesman, Cornelis Lely. Under his direction, a thirty-one-kilometre dam was completed in 1932 across the narrowest point in the Zuiderzee's inlet into the Netherlands. Using their time-tested methods, the Dutch began empoldering land along the edges of the newly formed inland sea—the Iésselmeer. The result was that between 1920 and 1963, the Dutch reclaimed nearly half of the sea's area, over 1,600 square kilometres, in four "polder" sections. The water in the sea—aided by the inflow of water from the Iéssel River and a complicated system of pumping stations and sluices—has slowly turned from brackish to fresh water in the past few decades and become an important source of water for the surrounding regions in times of drought.

The formation of the IJsselmeer and its polders meant that the Netherlands was much better able to handle the growing demands from other parts of Europe for the grains, fruits, vegetables and dairy products needed to satisfy their expanding markets. Leaders in the agricultural world who did not expect progress in salt water zones looked on with wonder. Men and women operating the small polder farms comprised of reclaimed land were talking about water management and erosion control and other sophisticated agricultural matters. Many wondered how much of the change in their way of life on the polders had come from the awful floods of 1953, when some of the rivers emptying into the Iésselmeer overflowed their banks.

At any rate, change had come and there was cause for rejoicing. Some of the "polder philosophers" were convinced that the change had come from improved water management and a more definite sense of pride in the unique local mix of geography and meteorology, which combined silt and salt water with an annual average rainfall of sixty-three centimetres a year—water as pure as any that ever left the clouds. Dutch farmers were now suddenly selling the bulbs and specialty cheese that people on the polders had previously been making just for themselves.

Tourists began coming to Holland in larger numbers, partly to see whether the Dutch water projects they had heard about were successful, but also simply to enjoy the understated beauty of the Dutch countryside. They gazed and marvelled at the wooden shoes fashioned right there on the polders, under the same roofs that sheltered the making of Gouda, Edam and many other kinds of cheese. And tourists were more or less mesmerised by the picturesque and photogenic Dutch wind-mills, whether they were in operation or not. The mill's owner would invariably want to make a speech to reinforce that the distinctive windmill was, indeed, a Dutch invention and that it had been improved immeasurably by the addition of a rotating turret to catch the wind from all directions. Most importantly, the windmill should be esteemed for its ability to generate power without consuming non-renewable resources.

Any discussion of the difficulties surrounding water in the

Netherlands demands a reference to the charming old story of the heroic Dutch boy, Hans Brinker. The story is a very familiar one and has many versions. The boy's name and some of the details are not always the same, but that does not seem to matter. The important thing is that when this author was growing up, Canadian students and teachers loved Hans. It was the young hero's resourcefulness, presence of mind and commitment that made him an enduring role model.

Even as a young boy, Hans Brinker recognized dangers when he saw them. As the story goes, Hans was walking the long trail home after dark beside the big dikes that held back the North Sea when he thought he heard a trickle. Pausing to investigate, he found that there was a small hole in the clay dike. If left unattended, the leak would soon be a gusher and flood the countryside. What was the resourceful country boy to do? He tried plugging the tiny hole with clay, but the water pressure forced the clay out as fast as he could push it in. Time was short. He had to work quickly. The lad discovered that his middle finger was just the right size to plug the hole. He inserted a finger and, as long as he kept it in the cavity, the North Sea was arrested. After a while Hans became cold and sleepy. He wanted to go home but he knew that to go would surely mean that the dike would be breached and the seawater gushing through by morning. Could he hang on until daylight? The gallant lad suffered but did not relent and the dikes survived. The story may only be a fiction, but that should not dilute its message.

Most of the Dutch boy's Canadian admirers were young people who read about his alleged acts of bravery in the pages of their public school readers. Not all of these students were of the same tender years as Hans when he performed the service of holding the dike through the long and cold Dutch night. One of them was the Russian-born Alberta politician, Henry Kroeger, who came to the Canadian prairies to farm in the memorable drought year of 1937. He became one of the province's foremost water conservationists and public servants. At the time of his death in 1987, he still held a seat in the Alberta Legislature where he had been a Minister of the Crown for many years. Some people saw fit to note that Mr. Kroeger had a perpetually serious expression, "almost an expression of anger." Donald Getty, Alberta Premier at the time, read the earnest face of his cabinet minister quite differently: "Tough, kindly and honest, you won't find them any greater." This was the man who stuck loyally by the Canadian dry belt. Kroeger went into provincial politics after farming and running a Massey Harris farm implement dealership. Repeatedly elected to the legislature, he became Minister of Transportation in Peter Lougheed's government and then, significantly, Chairman of the Alberta Water Resources Commission. The new chairman whispered to a friend soon after accepting the responsibilities of the Commission that he would be absent for a "week or two." When asked where he was going, he replied, "I have a date to sit under a Dutch windmill with Hans Brinker. We're going to talk about water."

Kroeger was probably a hundred years too late to see Hans in the flesh, but he had no doubts of finding enough Dutch history and water lore to keep him busy. For him, the quietly arranged trip would be a learning mission for which he would not need Brinker at all. He was then sixty-two years of age, and the trip was likely his last chance to see and study one country that had too much water, so he could apply the lessons he learned to the southern Canadian prairies, which didn't have enough. He knew he would find innovation in the Netherlands, which had the second highest population density in Europe, and where forty percent of the country was below sea level. Their shortage of space meant that they were still reclaiming agricultural land from the sea at costs that would have mortified Canadian and American farmers.

Kroeger felt he had to make the trip to the Netherlands, whether political colleagues saw the importance of it or not. For anybody dedicated to the conservation of soil and water, the journey's rewards could be expected to be great, and they were. Nor was it long after his return from Europe that the committees Kroeger chaired were being asked to consider seriously some of the "Old World" values and conservation principles which had greatly impressed him.

As a former dry land farmer with faith in irrigation where it was practical, Kroeger had long been convinced that his province should be making better use of its unparalleled water resources. Not everybody was equally convinced. The Alberta Advisory Committee on Water was at that time trying to give guidance to the provincial cabinet on the feasibility of diverting water from northern to southern Alberta via river basin transfer. Northern interests, having themselves been recent victims of moderate drought, did not welcome the notion of moving water from their lakes and rivers to the south at the taxpayers' expense. Kroeger was trying to maintain a balanced view but was convinced that the world had not seen the last of serious water shortages. He was of the view that the government of a province blessed with both soil and water in abundance had a moral duty to bring them together.

"We know we have the land," Kroeger said at a meeting of the Alberta Advisory Committee on Water in September, 1980.

> *We know we have the water; we know we have the climate. We also have the technology and equipment. And we're pretty sure we have the markets.... We think it is imprudent to talk about the high dollar cost of making our land more productive (by irrigation), and we use the restraining figure of $750 an acre that Peter Melnychuk developed for us. At the same time, in Europe we saw land being reclaimed from the sea at $12,000 an acre. You have to wonder how the Hollanders find the economics to allow a recovery price of $12,000 per acre when we are led to believe that $750 per acre is too much to pay for something that will make our land very much more productive.*

Asked later if he had been able to keep his date with Hans Brinker under the Dutch windmill, the serious Mr. Kroeger grinned broadly and answered, "No, Hans discovered a new leak in the dike, and he and his finger were too busy to get away."

PART V: SHARING WATER
Chapter Eleven: A Grandiose Transcontinental Waterway

I have little need to remind you that water has become one of our national concerns. Nearly everyone in this country in the past few years has experienced some problem caused by too much water when we do not want it, or too little water when we do want it. Farmers have had to haul water for stock in trucks from the cities. Some cities have had to haul water from farm ponds. New Yorkers for a time were asked to cut down the number of their baths, so low was the water in the reservoirs that served the metropolis. Homeowners in many places had to give up watering their lawns in order to husband municipal supplies. Some city councils have had warnings that the growth of their cities would be limited by the availability of water. An ample amount of clean water has become a factor in the location of new factories. The intrusion of salt water into overused wells is making insufferable the water in some underground reservoirs.

—Ezra Taft Benson,
U.S. Secretary of Agriculture, 1955.

Water reserves in Alberta: The Redwater Water Tower, 1956.
(Provincial Archives of Alberta, WS76)

It took the powerful forces of Nature many millions of years to shape the continental topography that would inspire a modern plan for the redistribution of British Columbia's huge surplus of fresh water to the western half of the North American continent. To Ralph Parsons, the ingenious water engineer who came to public prominence in the 1960s, the challenge was very clear: the $100 billion design that took shape in his research headquarters in Los Angeles was, in his estimation, the engineering "topic of the year."

Though it never reached fruition, the North American Water and Power Alliance (NAWAPA) deserves to be remembered as a child of grandiose and visionary science, born ahead of its time. If the North American population greatly increases at some point in the future, those marvellously inventive plans may be dusted off and looked at with renewed interest.

Born in New York in 1896, Parsons was a Californian by adoption and a global water guardian by instinct. Clearly, he enjoyed working on a "big playing field," one suffering from the periodic pains of water crisis. An older New York acquaintance of his, on hearing of the gargantuan scheme for the first time, was said to have remarked, "It's gotta be a Ralph Parsons stunt because nobody else would have the audacity to plan it, or the patience to pursue it. Ralph never made water flow uphill, but that's because nobody ever told him it couldn't be done."

It took the first half of the 1940s to convince North Americans that the hard times of the 1930s were really over. As the Second World War ground to a close, the thoughts of the populace were trained upon meaningful assurances that the peace which was being bought at such a terrible price in human blood would not be broken again. It was also directed towards the need to blunt the edge of drought that had brought suffering to large swathes of the population. The United Nations was created with high hopes and armed with powers to strengthen the cause of world peace. On the scientific and academic fronts, the world body was charged with combating the socio-economic problems that threatened the advance of human development. Ralph Parsons' resolve to join forces with Nature in overcoming some of its mistakes with water was therefore in keeping with the times.

Parsons' long experience in California, and his position as head of an engineering consulting company, came together in his grand design for diverting Canadian water in the early 1960s. The NAWAPA was a long-range plan to collect the surplus water of the Rocky Mountain region of British Columbia by damming most of the province's major rivers and redistributing it to the water-poor areas of Canada, the American West and Midwest, and northern Mexico. The heart of the system was to be an eight-hundred-kilometre-long storage reservoir in Canada in what is known as the Rocky Mountain Trench, at an elevation of nine hundred metres. The water from the trench would have provided water for a navigable waterway, unbroken between Vancouver on the Pacific coast to Duluth on Lake Superior. It would also have delivered irrigation water to users between Alberta and South Dakota, and boosted the water volume of the Great Lakes and the Mississippi River, improving navigation.

Believing his project to be sound and feasible, Parsons was ready to present it to the American, Mexican and Canadian public. He expected an enthusiastic reception from the American and Mexican agriculturalists, but his advisers cautioned him against taking the Canadians for granted. The wary northerners, they reasoned, would throw many impediments in the project's way, some of them inspired by politics, and others by a history of disappointment over previous cross-border deals they felt had favoured the United States. And their fears were correct because soon after Parsons' announcement, cautious Canadians were grumbling, "Any scheme with costs exceeding a hundred billion dollars will be sure to want more of my tax money, or be looking for a sneaky way of applying shortfalls to my public debt."

Parsons countered this complaint by underlining the economic soundness of his proposal: "I don't like deficits and debts any more than anybody else, but let's get it straight that a good investment is neither an extravagance nor a luxury. I shall be the most surprised person in California if, after good planning, this great asset cannot be added to the long list of water power projects coming to completion almost debt-free because of the early sales of power."

Supporters pointed out that, after generating its own power for pumping stations along the way, the developing system would be expected to yield in excess of $4 billion per year from the sale of power. In return for its water, the supplying area would receive payments in power or revenue from the sale of water or power sufficient to help rapidly repay the heavy capital costs.

Of the nine regional drainage basins accorded individual recognition in the NAWAPA prospectus of 1964, the Rocky Mountain Trench may have captured the biggest interest. It was a mountain valley traversed by many Canadians who had never considered how lovely it would look if it ever became an eight-hundred-kilometre lake framed by mountains. "The Rocky Mountain Trench," a Parsons report explained, "is a gorge containing the upper reaches of the Columbia, Fraser and Kootenay Rivers. By damming these rivers, a reservoir 500 miles long would be created, extending southerly to Flathead Lake in Montana. The setting of the Rocky Mountain Trench is one of mountain grandeur, being adjacent to Banff and Jasper National Parks. The large artificial lake should enhance the scenic and recreational assets of the region." It is possible that Canadian planners should have been considering the development of such a park with or without the supporting benefits of the NAWAPA.

The added supply of water that would have accompanied the NAWAPA programme would have increased the flow all the way to the Great Lakes. According to Parsons' estimates, it would have given the Lakes enough extra water to irrigate 140,000 square kilometres of Canadian farmland. He also claimed that delivering twenty million acre feet of water annually to Mexico would irrigate eight times as much land as the famous Aswan High Dam on the Nile River.

The spectacular water redistribution plan came to the full light of day in the spring of 1964, and by the late months of that year, Calgary and southern Alberta were awash with enthusiasm. D. A. Hansen, president of the Calgary Chamber of Commerce and one of the community's most vociferous supporters of the Parsons water programme, undertook to sponsor a monster promotional luncheon in December of that year, the thousand tickets for which sold out far in advance. Together with Hansen, prominent Parsons associates were in attendance at the meeting, all brimming with confidence. Albert W. Moore declared that the Calgary audience was the biggest and most heartening yet encountered on the NAWAPA tour, strongly suggesting approval in principle at least during this time of growing water shortages. The Great Lakes, he pointed out, were at their lowest levels in 104 years, while other parts of the continent were affected by floods and pollution. Moore estimated that the population of Canada and the United States would double to 400 million by the year 2000, and that demand for water would double by 1980 and triple by the year 2000. "The problem of water supply must be resolved on a practical rather than a political basis," he added. "Nature did not take political boundaries into consideration when resource treasures were being bestowed on this continent."

In presenting the NAWAPA, Moore admitted he was well aware of the enormity of the obstacles it needed to overcome: political considerations involving international agreements, and innumerable engineering and financial hurdles required attention. The task would not be easy. According to Moore, thirty percent of the total cost of $100 billion would be spent in Canada. The NAWAPA would provide Canada with an annual income of over two-billion dollars while furnishing thirty million kilowatts of electrical power in addition to the thirty million kilowatts required for pumping within the system.

It should come as no surprise that the Calgary Chamber of Commerce was extremely impressed. But there are two sides to every coin. When Calgarians read their Herald on December 16, 1964, they were confronted by an editorial critiquing the NAWAPA. Instead of rushing to the scene with the speed of a fire brigade, the writers offered words of sober advice:

> *For Canadians, the proposal outlined in Calgary recently for a $100 billion continental water distribution scheme has one overriding drawback: it would transfer effective control of Canada's main river system to the United States. No amount of money could recompense this country for such a loss. The appeal to Canada is likely to be made on the high level that water is a continental resource which should be utilized on a continental basis, and also on the more practical level that the plan would involve the spending of billions of dollars annually in Canada. The latter type of appeal is likely to be the siren song most likely to entrap Canada into becoming water-boy in perpetuity to the US Most people will realize that water isn't any more a continental resource than iron ore, or forests, or oil.*
>
> *A plan like the NAWAPA scheme could therefore permanently limit the growth of the Canadian Prairies, for example, which are expected to be facing a water shortage in forty or fifty years. It would seem far better for Canada*

to start work right now devising its own water
storage and distribution plan which would serve
Canadian need first.

Confronted by reasoned and lucid opposition such as this, the widely-heralded NAWAPA, with its staggering cost estimates, was destined to flounder. Its tenure on the political stage was melodramatic and brief. But it provoked worthwhile debate on a subject long ignored. Many began to wonder why Canadians shouldn't start work on devising their own water storage and distribution system, which would serve Canada with Canadian water. Canadians were interested in maintaining their great water inheritance, but remained unsure as to policy direction.

And sure enough, Alberta, which found itself particularly rich in fresh water wealth, led the western provinces in exploring ways to utilize the benefits of its water treasure. Albertans were reminded that eighty-seven percent of their northward flow of stream water ended up unused in the Arctic Ocean, while eighty percent of the provincial population, representing a large share of the water market, lived within two hundred kilometres of the American border.

The Alberta government was well aware that increased water reserves would improve the position of irrigationists in southern Alberta and increase the security of residents in Fort Macleod and Lethbridge who needed water for domestic purposes. On January 28, 1966, less than fourteen months after the NAWAPA's promotional luncheon in Calgary, a new course was set for water distribution on the Canadian prairies. Harry

Strom, Alberta's Minister of Agriculture, announced the construction of the Three Rivers or Oldman River Dam, a few miles north of Pincher Creek. Expecting this proposal to be well received, he announced dozens of other provincial water projects, all of which seemed to clarify a new course for water management. The new policies deserved a new name as distinctive as Parsons' NAWAPA. As a result, PRIME, or the Prairie Rivers Improvement and Management Evaluation, was born. It saw as its first mandate the stabilization of water supplies in the Lethbridge Northern Irrigation District.

Of the more than fifty water projects chosen for approval, there were river diversions, watershed rehabilitation, flood control measures and irrigation dams of various sizes and shapes. These projects were certainly sufficient enough in scope to change the water-deployment scene in Alberta. The provincial government appeared to have seized a national role in water initiatives. Some of it resembled a replay of the William Pearce scheme to channel water from foothills rivers, including the Red Deer, to natural storage basins such as Sullivan Lake, north of Hanna, Alberta. In retrospect, many of the PRIME projects have not advanced on schedule, and some may never be completed. But some did succeed and, in the words of that "great high priest" of irrigation and water conservation, Henry Kroeger, the projects the million-dollar PRIME programme brought into service were more deserving of praise than the multibillion dollar NAWAPA plan that never got off the ground.

Chapter Twelve: California and the Dream of Icebergs

Then ho, brothers, ho,
To California go.
There's plenty of gold in the world we're told,
On the banks of the Sacramento.
...The gold is thar, most anywaar,
And they dig it out with an iron bar.

> — Jesse Hutchinson, during the
> California Gold Rush, 1848-49

A lthough the world may always boast a sufficiency of drinking water for all basic needs, by the time six billion humans and the rest of the earth's creatures take what they need, those adequate supplies may become inadequate. Poor distribution can lead to serious problems, and minor shortages, especially in regions of the world grappling with poverty and overpopulation, can have tragic results. Water scarcity has posed problems for rich and poor alike. Even the extremely prosperous state of California has had to contend with shortages of water.

Proud of the phenomenal growth of its population and industry, California has long struck a precarious balance between water reserves and the soaring growth of its water

The Columbia Icefields, 1961.
(Provincial Archives of Alberta, PA 1778/1)

consumption. Name almost any high-risk water gamble that many government bodies would prefer to avoid at all costs, and chances are that California has at some time faced that test and passed it. "Californians," many outsiders have remarked, "are born gamblers."

Rival states have long suspected the "Golden State" of employing an unending series of magic spells to attract citizens and prosperity: the Gold Rush, the booms in real estate and oil, the boon of the motion picture industry, and the concerted growth of irrigation and agricultural output. In 1848, James Marshall discovered gold at Sutter's Hill in the Sacramento Valley, and he was followed by tens of thousands of fortune-crazed adventurers. The population of the new state of California was still under one-hundred-thousand in 1850, but not for much longer. Its dizzying population increase to thirty-million by 1995 must have few equals.

As California's population soared, so did its water needs and the difficulties in delivering it. Los Angeles, by far the biggest city in California, has contributed the most to water history over the years. Its annual precipitation is a paltry thirty-eight centimetres, compared with fifty-six centimetres for San Francisco. It may be that the sprawling city demonstrated what any city of its size would elect to do if faced with the threat of serious water shortages. The city's policy was to secure contracts on unclaimed water supplies from the nearby Sierra Madre and areas further afield. As it turned out, large volumes were obtained from Owens River on the east side of the Sierra Nevada, from Mona Lake, more than 500 kilometres away, and from the Colorado River, 725 kilometres distant. Remoteness, in light of necessity, was becoming less and less of an obstacle.

Locating the necessary water supplies for Californian cities big and small was added to the more traditional activities that had earlier attracted people to the region, such as hunting for gold, fertile land, oil or wild game. One distinction that sets water apart from the rest of these resources is that the excessive rise in the cost of water will not be accepted by the public as a reason for discontinuance of production. Distinct from any other resource, water is likely to make its own rules in the marketplace.

Californians have recently had to look even further afield for new sources of fresh water, and the search has become more arduous and costly. New contracts for the purchase of new supplies brought brief tides of rejoicing to Los Angeles, at least until the enormous costs were received and assessed. Not long ago, the big city reportedly faced a thiry-eight-million dollar annual debt for the purchase of water from the heavily used Colorado River, which forms the eastern border of the state, and the San Joaquin River to the north. At about the same time as these big invoices for water were being publicly ventilated, the state governor found it expedient to announce another multimillion dollar programme for the maintenance and repair of water transportation facilities. The total cost was staggering. Taxpayers muttered that it was time to consider ways of recycling waste water and sewage, whether the idea was popular or not.

California's huge and complex fresh water system, refined so skilfully by natural forces, does not make many mistakes. As its magnificent centrepiece, the dignified Sierra Nevada sits like a dowager queen in a high court, judging, as it were, the merits of bold water experiments. Californians have invented new techniques in irrigation such as "drip irrigation," which involves minimal water application to the roots for upward percolation. Methods of irrigating agricultural land with sewage and recycled sewage water have been duly tested, but have met with varying degrees of public enthusiasm.

California is the North American pioneer in bringing resourcefulness to the search for water. The most marginal water sources have been studied, such as the minuscule deposits of water on grass or clover after a heavy night of dew or fog. Some found ways of recovering a few cupfuls with the help of blankets or sheets. If the indigenous peoples who employed these practices believed that tiny amounts of truly pure water were worth the effort, then they probably were.

And then there is the whole question of refining seawater or any water unsuitable for either irrigation or human consumption. Advanced studies of desalination plants grew out of this to determine which, if any, could be operated at acceptable costs. Santa Barbara was one of the first cities in the state to operate its own desalination plant. Constructed on San Nicholas Island in 1991, the plant was expected to supply 55,000 litres of drinking water per day at a cost of just under a twenty-five cents a litre. The relatively high cost is still the principal obstacle to the construction of similar plants. Isolating and containing the raw seawater is not particularly expensive, but the power required to effect the separation of water and salt is generally high enough to make users think twice about investing heavily in desalination.

Renewed criticism of California water policies came along with the severe drought of 1987-92. The most vociferous critics were the irrigation farmers who were told to reduce their use of public water. Anybody using the public supply felt the effects of the curtailments, but the irrigators, who had been enjoying the biggest share of "government water" for years, had the most to say. The main targets of their criticism were the many large residential swimming pools in Los Angeles and other parts of southern California. It was estimated there were more than 600,000 private pools (each averaging 90,000 litres in size) in California, three-quarters of them in the southern half of the state. Irrigators and stockmen claimed they represented an extravagant use of water and believed they should have primary claims. At about the same time, the Los Angeles Department of Water and Power added fuel to the flame by demanding a twenty-five percent reduction in water use for household purposes, levying heavy fines for those who failed to comply.

Despite their usually unshakeable optimism, Californians have acknowledged renewed difficulties in coping with their record increases in water demands. "But don't be impatient," a native son of Los Angeles was known to have said. "We've had water problems before and we'll fix them again."

One of those who came forward with a solution was O.B. Lassiter. His idea was daring, almost unbelievable. It may have been a reflection of the company Lassiter was keeping during his winters in California, but he believed that the first polar ice water would be delivered to that state in his lifetime. His prediction went something like this: "Just let the Los Angeles people feel a bit more of the stress of thirst and you'll see a captive Antarctic iceberg being guided towards that city to furnish a supply of the best drinking water in the world."

Lassiter rates as an agricultural pioneer in California and Alberta. What he witnessed in both places was an unusual resourcefulness in adjusting to problems of water supply. The Old Testament prophet, Joel, may have had something to offer: "Your old men shall dream dreams and your young men shall see visions" (Joel 2:28). Lassiter was the old man "dreaming dreams," but the young men have not produced the visible iceberg in tow, at least not yet!

John Isaac of the Scripps Institute of Oceanography in California appears to have been the first academic to advance the idea of isolating free-floating icebergs and guiding them to coastal regions where the need for pure water was most urgent. The earliest public reaction was mixed. Some greeted it with derisive laughter. Newspaper cartoonists, for instance, drew satiric pictures of California's Iceberg Navy of the future. But as the need for fresh water grew, so did this bold vision for moving real Antarctic icebergs.

Lassiter had the conscience of a conservationist. Lacking formal training in science, he had, as he described it, "the patience of a well-digger and the stamina of a glacier climber." His special passion for ice-rafting in the Antarctic waters aside, he and his cronies loved to speculate about capturing errant icebergs. Many of the ideas put forward by Dr. John Isaac of the Scripps Institute in 1957 were still recognized as feasible and attractive by Lassiter in his 1973 report.

The most popular model for moving the ice was "iceberg

trains," which consisted of between four and six bergs of selected shape and size, hitched in tandem fashion. The front unit carried motors and other heavy equipment, and acted as the "locomotive." Travelling speed was about two kilometres per hour. By travelling twenty-four hours a day, around two thousand kilometres could be covered in forty days. Contemporary readers might attempt to imagine what one of those average-sized bergs would look like when anchored in a harbour beside a busy city. That part of the city would immediately be cool; the hope was that melting would be slow enough to keep thawing to a minimum. This source of high-quality drinking water would probably survive for at least one full year.

California critics showed some impatience with the plan. "We are convinced that iceberg ice will give us excellent drinking water, but when are we going to be realistic about the costs of delivering icebergs to our shore? The best drink in the world isn't much good to us if we can't pay for it." Perhaps those who aspired to be the first trial-and-error salesmen of ice in history were not sure of the figures either. Their iceberg water would have to be less expensive than desalination plants in order to be a success. Pressed for an answer, the two Californians who were responsible for this latest scheme reported that it would cost less than a million dollars for a tug with which to deliver an iceberg, but that the berg would have the water potential of "207 billion gallons [930 billion litres] of delivery, and be worth, on a good market, $5.8 million" (Magazine Resources, January, 1970). The project then looked "too good," and confidence suffered. Again, the thirsty people continued to wait.

World water statistics may seem extremely dull when left unexplained, but they often illustrate points of deep importance. The reader, when informed that the world's supply of water totals 1.4 billion cubic kilometres, might conclude that these are simply big figures offering no justification whatsoever for any attempt to memorize them. But memorization is not as difficult or ridiculous as it first appears. There is great consolation in the knowledge that the world's water will never decrease with use, there being the same quantity on the earth today as there was thousands of years ago. Clearly, water reserves are constantly on the move or changing form: what is fresh rainwater today may be ice tomorrow and steam or fog the next day.

As mentioned earlier, most of the world's supply of water, about ninety-seven percent, is in the oceans and is too salty for human consumption. Humanity must find its domestic supplies in the remaining three percent. There remains, however, roughly two percent of drinkable water in the glaciers and polar icecaps. This is not the kind of distribution that most people would anticipate, but it does show the central importance of the ice at the poles.

Polar ice will attract many who will wish to exploit it when it becomes economically viable to market it and will need friends with an environmental concern for its safety to ensure that it is carried out responsibly. As long as the sales of ice and water are restricted to glacial chunks and bergs, other losses due to waste will not be greater than in the course of natural processes, and not likely to induce more extensive natural melting. But any disturbance that would start a warming trend should be looked upon as presenting a disastrous threat of flooding and swollen rivers. Protection of Nature's ice cover should be seen as one of the conservationist's important responsibilities.

Chapter Thirteen: The International Joint Commission: Negotiating Solutions

Property in water long antedated property in land in the arid lands of antiquity. Property rights were associated primarily with the use of water—first for drinking, next for irrigation. Mohammed saw water as an object of religious charity. He declared that free access to water was the right of every Moslem community and that no Moslem should want for it. The precept of the Holy Koran: "No one can refuse surplus water without sinning against Allah and against Man," was the cornerstone of a whole body of social traditions and of regulations governing the ownership, use and protection of water supplies.

All persons who shared rights to a watercourse were held responsible for its maintenance and cleaning. The whole community was responsible for the care of large watercourses. Cleaning was to start at the head of the stream or canal, descending in order to each watercourse family. All users shared the costs in proportion to their irrigation needs.

—Bernard Frank, 1955

A Pilot Boat on the vast St. Lawrence River c. 1922.
(Glenbow Museum Archives, NA-5095-1)

It is an oft-repeated boast that the Canadian-American reserves of fresh water represented by the Great Lakes and the St. Lawrence River are the largest in the world, akin to claiming the biggest diamond ever discovered. This pride in the Great Lakes is certainly not mistaken, though boasting about drinkable water in a world where supplies often fall short of needs is not in good taste at any time.

Nor does it mean that the mighty and majestic St. Lawrence really dwarfs all other rivers in the world. The Mackenzie and Mississippi, both North American rivers, are bigger than the St. Lawrence, and the volume of flow of all three is surpassed by the mammoth Amazon. Nevertheless, the St. Lawrence has world-class status and has inspired the praise and pride of many admirers, especially since the St. Lawrence Seaway was opened in 1959.

Each of the five Great Lakes has distinctive characteristics in size and depth. Together they present a water surface of about 246,000 square kilometres. Lake Superior is by far the biggest, broadest, deepest and most treacherous. With roughly 52,000 square kilometres of water surface, it represents one-third of the total Great Lakes area, and its unique position in commerce and export, particularly in grain from Western Canada, makes it of prime national importance.

All who share that pride should seek to understand the historical and geological secrets of the Great Lakes. The Vikings who established settlements on the Atlantic coast a thousand years ago may have visited them, but no traces have been found that would confirm this. The next European to display more interest in exploration than piracy was John Cabot, a Venetian, who sailed for North America in 1497 under the English flag for King Henry VII. He was delighted to find excellent fishing at the mouth of the St. Lawrence. After reporting to his sovereign, Cabot was instructed to return the following year. There seems to have been a mishap, though, as the great explorer never returned to England to take up this commission.

The next few decades found Jacques Cartier and other French explorers on the St. Lawrence, probing inland. In 1541, Cartier navigated as far as the Indian village of Stadacona and wintered there on the future site of Quebec City. Not far away, he planted a wooden cross, thereby claiming the country for France. Cartier was a man of boundless energy. He seems to have covered the lower St. Lawrence with exploration in mind, but was unsuccessful in getting to the western reaches of the river where he had hoped to find China. His visit to Hochelaga in 1541, the Native village on the site of present-day Montréal, was to have been extended westward in the spring but his efforts were suspended.

Samuel de Champlain was an early visitor on Lake Huron. He was by nature a colonizer more than an explorer, although inclined to travel the unknown country with his friend, Étienne Brûlé. An eccentric fellow, Brûlé was welcomed by the Huron Indians and spent the latter part of his life with them. Brûlé was probably the first of his race to see Lake Ontario and Lake Erie, as well as the country north of Lake Superior. He likely died with the Hurons, to whom he remained loyal, and historians have speculated that he may have been murdered by the

Iroquois, traditional Huron enemies. What a misfortune that Brûlé's life as a European living with the aboriginal peoples was never incorporated into his own writing! Indeed, there is little consolation in the thought that hundreds more like him have left no written record.

Even the Great Lakes themselves are capable of being mysterious and misleading. For example, the floor and shorelines of the lakes are incrementally rising. In technical circles, this phenomenon is known as "isostatic rebound." The rebound of the floor of the lakes is not something that can be studied with the naked eye, but must be measured in mere centimetres per year. The slow rate of these changes aside, the gradual rising action is thought to be the result of the incredible weight exerted on the region by glacial ice during one of the Ice Ages: the ice that once covered today's Thunder Bay has been estimated to have been one to three kilometres deep. The ice might have indeed reached such weights that it caused the earth's crust to bend, stretch and sag. When the ice melted and the burden disappeared, the slightly elastic crust began to recover all or part of its former levels. This theory has been offered increasingly to account for the peculiar geological characteristics of the Great Lakes basin. Scientists with a special interest in Northern Studies are quite familiar with isostatic rebound, since there is widely recognized evidence of rising coastlines and ancient gravel beaches extending far beyond the present-day shorelines of Hudson's Bay.

Nearly fifty million people live within the drainage area of the Great Lakes, involving two nations separated by a razor-thin boundary line which divides seven American states from the province of Ontario. It should come as no surprise, then, that the water has posed administrative problems for governments on both sides of the border. One solution has been to create co-operative joint bodies, the most important of these being the International Joint Commission (IJC). The oldest intergovernmental body between Canada and the United States, it was set up in 1909 to deal with such matters as pollution in the shared water resources. Progress has been made in a variety of areas, but it never seems fast enough. At its worst moments in the 1970s and 80s, Lake Erie, for instance, had all the symptoms of a dead lake.

By 1992, Environment Canada reported that the Great Lakes and the St. Lawrence River were having serious difficulty cleansing themselves and sustaining life: "Various species of fish suffer from tumours and lesions, and their reproductive capacities are decreasing. Populations of fish-consuming birds and mammals also seem to be on the decline. Of the ten most highly valued species of fish in Lake Ontario, seven have now almost totally vanished." They went on to attribute this to the over 360 chemical compounds that had been identified in the Great Lakes. Many were resilient toxic chemicals—alkylated lead, benzopyrene, DDT, mercury and mirex—which had already seriously damaged the aquatic ecosystem and were potentially dangerous to humans.

While acknowledging some of its limitations, the recent ninetieth anniversary of the Commission deserved to be celebrated. It has been a remarkably effective institution, working to resolve quarrelsome water-related differences between Canadians and Americans not only in the Great Lakes but all along their border. In one particularly interesting instance in Western Canada, though, the IJC benefited from the work done by a local group before the Commission had been formed.

After the turn of the century, disputes flared up over the water use of the St. Mary's and Milk Rivers in southern Alberta. Both international rivers, they flow into Canada southwest of Lethbridge, the Milk eventually re-crossing the border near the boundary between Alberta and Saskatchewan. Not willing to wait for Ottawa and Washington to act, local leaders like Canada's William Pearce persuaded a number of residents to serve as a board of councillors to oversee disputes over water usage.

Confronted with a wide range of issues, Pearce provided the local board with wise and sound direction and an honest transnational concern for fair water allocations, pollution control and conservation. The chief concern was that interest in irrigation was growing rapidly on both sides of the border. In Montana, especially, water users were inclined to divert irrigation water from the Canadian part of both the St. Mary and Milk Rivers at a time when safeguards were lax and any review of ethics left for later discussions. Pearce advocated that irrigation water in the two rivers be considered a "one water system to be allocated to users by negotiation."

In 1908, the United States Supreme Court ruled that aboriginal people living near the Milk River had a primary claim on its water. Most Montana irrigators saw the ruling as a threat to their security, and were thus anxious to negotiate with their Canadian counterparts. In less than a year, the International

Joint Commission was passed into law and water users on both sides of the border felt a new sense of security. With new clarity and firmness, the IJC entrenched the earlier "unofficial" principles of justice in allocation and pollution control.

Time puts a new face on many of humanity's creations and activities. An examination of the IJC's long and active history draws this point into focus. The IJC's fiftieth anniversary in 1959 coincided with the opening of the St. Lawrence Seaway. The Seaway was the product of more than five years of heavy construction and stood on completion as the most costly river development of its kind undertaken in the western hemisphere. This momentous occasion was marked by the presence of Queen Elizabeth II, and American president Dwight D. Eisenhower. Members of the IJC accepted the Seaway's completion as a new mandate to fight pollution, and were prepared to exercise more rather than less care in safeguarding water reserves. Rejecting complacency, the IJC called for greater determination in preserving one of the planet's most vital fresh water resources. Another forty years on, the international body is still upholding the same ideals of fairness and co-operation with respect to water that it has demonstrated in the past.

Chapter Fourteen: Controversy On the Columbia River

*It is with rivers as it is with people; the greatest
are not always the most agreeable nor the best
to live with.*

—Henry van Dyke

The Columbia River—big, twisty and picturesque—appears at times like a crawling
monster that is not sure where it wants to go.
After leaving its headwaters in southwestern British
Columbia's relatively small Lake Columbia, it can be seen
flowing briskly north as if intending to head to the Arctic
Ocean. But instead of continuing on such a course, it turns
sharply around and flows south towards the town of
Revelstoke. After passing through the Arrow Lakes, the big
river, growing ever larger, enters the United States south of
Trail, British Columbia. It finally meets the Pacific Ocean at a
point near the city of Portland, Oregon, having travelled 1,970
kilometres from its headwaters.

The great Canadian explorer David Thompson was to travel the full length of the Columbia River, mapping it meticu-
lously all the way. An English orphan, he entered the North

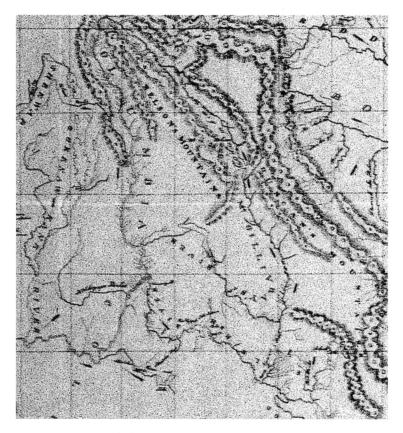

David Thompson's map of the Columbia River.
(Glenbow Museum Archives, G3465/1814/T469/1906)

American fur trade in 1784 at the age of fourteen, serving first with the Hudson's Bay Company and then the North West Company. By the early nineteenth century, Thompson was recognized as the finest mapmaker in the country, and made his headquarters at Rocky Mountain House.

Travelling exclusively by canoe, Thompson was often accompanied by his wife, Charlotte Small, an aboriginal woman, and most of their thirteen children. He was probably not anticipating competition for the distinction and land rights traditionally conceded to the first explorer to reach a landmark. Doubtless, then, Thompson was extremely surprised and disappointed on July 15, 1811 to discover that the agents of the wealthy American trader, John Jacob Astor, had reached the river's mouth to the sea just a few days before his arrival. The New York men had already staked their claim to the promising trading site. Nevertheless, Thompson had his maps as a proper compensation for his efforts, and knew there were many other potentially good sites for trading posts and forts on the river upstream. When Thompson decided shortly after that journey to retire in the St. Lawrence valley, it was estimated that he had covered not less than eighty thousand stream kilometres in Western Canada, and had mapped every one of them.

The Americans were also to be the first to display a business interest in the irrigation and power potential of the Columbia. For them, the stream's long stretches of wild water that powerfully swept past mountain obstacles conjured up visions of great economic reward. Canadians, on the other hand, were thinking mainly about fishing and the preservation of one of the best salmon spawning habitats in the world.

To gain the best advantage in their scheme for development, the Americans needed a series of dams on the Columbia's Canadian side to furnish vast water reservoirs and effective flood control. Even during the preliminary planning stages, governments on both sides of the border recognized the mechanical, ecological and political complexities of the new problems they were facing. They wisely agreed to ask the International Joint Commission to conduct a study and make recommendations. This was precisely what it had been set up to do. Canadians felt reassured and found further comfort when General Andrew McNaughton, a distinguished soldier, scientist, and public servant, was appointed to serve as the area chairman of the Canadian contingent. It was McNaughton, in his unrelenting advocacy of Canadian interests, who was to emerge as one of the principal critics of the Columbia River Treaty. McNaughton was convinced that the treaty ran counter to Canadian interests. Even under the most favourable circumstances, McNaughton told his friends, history had demonstrated that the coercion of a community into sharing its water reserves was one of the surest forerunners of ill will, hostility and even war. He believed the Columbia River Treaty held the seeds of both dissatisfaction and conflict.

Born at Moosamin, Northwest Territories in 1887, McNaughton had grown up on the Canadian prairies where water was always a challenge and an issue. During his many years on the International Joint Commission, some of them as chairman of the Canadian negotiating team, he was probably the best informed public servant on water issues in the entire country. Nobody knew friction and debate better than General

McNaughton, who could look back on many years of exposure to the Commission's heated discussions. Collegues began to remark upon his growing impatience and crustiness as his tenure of service with that international body lengthened.

McNaughton may have been the first Canadian engaged in the Columbia River water discussions bold enough to criticize the United States' handling of water issues, alleging their failure to honour early commitments. His reservations about the Columbia River Treaty had grown over time and he now believed that it signalled the loss of Canadian control over its own water resources. While sovereignty issues were important for McNaughton, it was the environmental ones which were the most compelling of all. He was convinced that the long series of dams already in place along the Columbia was ruining what was reputed to be the best salmon spawning riverbed in the world.

McNaughton's concerns about the effects dams could have on river habitat were in many ways before their time. Environmental issues and the border-crossing politics of water were to come to the fore in the late 1960s as the effects from another British Columbia dam project were being felt downstream in Alberta. Begun in 1968, the huge Gordon M. Shrum hydro-electric dam on the Peace River was blamed for the environmental grief suffered in the Lake Athabasca delta region of Alberta. The delta owed its existence to two big rivers, the Athabasca flowing in from the south and the Peace from the west. Coming together and looking like a grand mix of small lakes, streams and varied wetlands at the west end of Lake Athabasca, the resulting water habitat was a haven for fishing and hunting by the native peoples of the area. But, somehow, the Gordon M. Shrum Dam's planners and promoters—who included Premier William Andrew Cecil Bennett and later his son Premier William Richards Bennett—had overlooked or seriously underestimated the devastation that would accompany the loss of flow from the Peace River: the fall in muskrat population, the rampant growth of willow shrubs that would choke out other vegetation, and the disastrous effects on fishing.

The environmental concerns of thirteen engineers, biologists, geographers and social scientists were set out in a 1970 brief submitted to Prime Minister Pierre Trudeau and Alberta Premier Harry Strom:

> *The 1,000 square mile [2,500 square kilometre] delta of the Peace River and Athabasca River near Fort Chipewyan, Alberta comprises a unique ecological system of lakes and rivers. More than half the area lies within Wood Buffalo National Park.... Recent studies show that profound changes have taken place because the regulation of the Peace River by the dam in British Columbia has robbed the delta of the spring floods that are necessary to fill its many lakes and maintain the water levels in Lake Athabasca. These changes will become permanent unless appropriate action is taken soon.*

The Peace River Dam provided a bitter lesson about the dangers that could follow the mismanagement of massive hydro-electric projects.

The Columbia River Treaty was signed on January 17, 1961 after more than twelve years of discussion and debate. By this time, the American portion of the river was marked by a dozen or more hydro-electric facilities. The Americans badly needed more water for their existing power installations, and better flood management of upstream water. To accommodate these needs, Canada agreed to construct three dams on Canadian soil at Mica Creek, the Arrow Lakes and Duncan Lake. The total cost was to be around $400 million. The designated dams were built, all of them for storage and not to generate power as many Canadian residents had probably hoped. Additional Canadian water, everybody understood, would help to generate more power and profits for American producers who in turn knew they would have to pay Canadians for the increased power productivity. The block of electric power returned to Canada annually would be like a rental fee for intrusion into Canadian water resources.

The determination of the amount paid to Canada for this extra power would not be simple to work out, either. It took years to agree on the details. In the end, however, Canada was to receive sixty-four million US dollars per year, plus a block of hydro power based on the estimated downstream increases in power production resulting from the greater flow of Canadian water. In return, Canada gave in to American pressure and agreed to build an additional auxiliary storage dam on the Kootenay River.

Three years later, British Columbia negotiators successfully lobbied the Canadian government for permission to sell their entire share of these American power benefits back to the United States. The $250 million deal was to be in effect for the forthcoming thirty years, or half life of the Columbia River Treaty.

British Columbia, needless to say, was to enjoy a spell of great prosperity and William Andrew Cecil Bennett and his Social Credit government fared no less well in popularity. Bennett, who held the British Columbia premier's office for twenty distinguished years, was a New Brunswicker by birth, and a hardware merchant by occupation. A former finance minister, he had traditionally held a tight rein on provincial expenditures. In the years that followed the signing of the Columbia River deal, Premier Bennett was able to boast that British Columbia was the only province in Canada to be debt-free. The federal government and most provincial governments at the time were letting their public debts soar like break-away balloons.

Bennett's grasp of politics and fiscal realities was more adept than has been widely recognized. His American counterparts in the extended negotiations would probably agree that nobody could "cut an apple into five quarters" as well as he could. And for patience and endurance in negotiations, he proved to be a proper match for the Americans who sat opposite him. Making the best use of international water is always a delicate and difficult operation. To be both useful and just in the supervision of public water, the good servant needs the judgement of King Solomon and the balancing skills of a circus acrobat.

VI. WATERSHED CHOICES
Chapter Fifteen:
Using Water: Edmonton Versus Calgary

Flow on, flow on, dear Yarrow stream,
Your rippling voice is sweet to me;
Your grassy banks are still as green
As when I bade farewell to thee.

Near four score years have dimmed my sight,
Have slowed my gait and aged me sore,
But still you are as young and bright—
The Yarrow of the days of yore.

—James Cowan, 1888

C algary and Edmonton, proud cities of Alberta, have much in common. Considered together, they represent more than half the population of the "Foothills Province," and have drawn distinction as well as wealth from the nearby resources of soil, water, oil, natural gas, coal, mountain grandeur and unspoiled wilderness. A Calgary Board of Trade official once insisted upon adopting and extending that list of natural gifts by adding "the world's

Bringing home the water supply in Irma, Alberta c. 1909.
(Glenbow Museum Archives, NA-3028-3)

best hockey players." Edmonton's Board of Trade responded by adding to its own list of natural distinctions "the world's second biggest liars."

Albertans know very well that there are no laws against boasting and that admonitions directed at exaggeration are impotent. "Peace and good will" is a lovely concept until filed away for the hockey season, or withdrawn from the Calgary-Edmonton debating agenda, when discussion is likely to expose the inflammatory debate as to which city may rightly claim the title of "Oil Capital."

Water transportation was once seen as favourable in both the Calgary and Edmonton areas, where water volume was sufficient to support rafts, canoes and river boats. Edmonton could claim the bigger and more versatile river in the North Saskatchewan. Calgary, with the Bow and Elbow, could claim the two highly scenic foothills streams. Although not suitable for bulk shipping, these two streams came together in Calgary, and, after embracing like first cousins, flowed on to become part of the broad South Saskatchewan River.

The community of Edmonton owed its origin to the fur trade. If Calgary had a debt of origin, it was to be the illicit "fire water" whiskey brought by Americans to trade with the native peoples of the prairie region. The defiant traders from Montana were followed into the Canadian southwest by the North West Mounted Police, who were under order to end the booze business. Despite their dissimilar roots, supplies of good water were essential for both the new communities of Calgary and Edmonton. The abundance of water of uncertain quality was evident enough, but the first question that most newcomers asked was, "Where does one look to find water that is safe to drink?"

Prior to 1903, Edmonton's residents obtained their water supplies by the horse and tank method, though a few fortunate individuals had wells. Fire protection was provided by a volunteer fire brigade using buckets and hand pumps. There were also large underground wooden tanks in various parts of the town, which were filled with water hauled in tanks from the river. These underground tanks were often of limited usefulness for fire-fighting as they required diligent refilling and were often found empty just when they were urgently needed.

A full-fledged waterworks system began to fall into place in 1902 when the Town of Edmonton passed Bylaw No. 220, authorizing an expenditure of $140,000 for the installation of a water and sewage system, all of which would be on the north side of the river and east of 102nd Street. The water system was laid out during the summer and fall of 1903: ten kilometres of water mains, eight kilometres of sewer mains, one-hundred buildings serviced by water and fifty fire hydrants. Unfortunately, the city showed a considerable deficit in the first year on a revenue of $2,116.32 and expenditures of $3,147.24.

Calgary, following its incorporation as a town in 1884, improved its water position somewhat when John Brennan, who owned two horses and a wagon, agreed to obtain a galvanized iron water tank. In doing so, he became the town's first free-enterprise water man, offering drinkable water from his own well close to the river. He would visit his customers once a week and fill family water barrels for twenty-five cents each, an expenditure not to be taken lightly in those days.

Residents at Fort Edmonton in the same years could buy water from a privately-owned well in the river valley at exactly the same price as in Calgary. In both towns, nobody raised the fears of a cartel that would push up the price of water, but big changes were coming, nevertheless. The first important administrative action following Calgary's incorporation was the appointment of a Fire, Water and Light Committee which recommended the purchase of two 135,000 litre water tanks for the central business area, mainly for the use and support of the newly-formed bucket fire brigade. The committee also encouraged the formation and incorporation of the Calgary Gas and Waterworks Company to operate a water supply franchise and utility in the town. Formed in 1887, and including prominent businessmen like James A. Lougheed, Alexander Lucas and P.M. Garity, the company agreed to commence operations by constructing a waterworks system no later than September 1, 1890.

A pump house was built and a steam-powered pump installed. The principal mains were laid in a generally eastward direction from an inlet near the Eau Claire Lumber Company's mill on the Bow River. The company had good intentions, but the obstacles to success were many. By the target date of 1890, the company's capital debt was $87,000 and its assets about $85,000. The town council, perhaps feeling somewhat guilty, promptly bought the company's assets, thereby liquidating the debt and leaving the town with a half-complete water system.

The city's water specialists went on to create the Glenmore Reservoir, a lake so exquisitely beautiful that it won the highest praise from many international observers. The foothills setting and snow-covered mountain background were Nature's contribution.

The consulting engineers recognized urgent needs for waterworks expansion and change in the system's man-made components, and drew attention to extensive bacterial contamination in both the Bow and Elbow Rivers. That in itself was like a call for a new supply system; it led to the purchase of six square kilometres of land for the main basin, and finally the construction of the familiar Glenmore Dam, Reservoir and water treatment facilities at a total cost of $4 million. Calgary mayor Andrew Davison turned the ceremonial first sod on the project on July 26, 1930, and was present to see the new system in operation about two-and-a-half years later.

Almost at once Calgary had a lake-size reservoir holding up to 21.5 million cubic litres, but it came with new concerns about human safety if the dam were to break and flood the city. Conscious of that fear, one of the consulting engineers, William Gore, reassured home owners on the lower side of the dam. A City of Calgary brochure released shortly after the dam's completion stated that, with the dam's position immediately above the densely populated city, the structure was designed not only from the standpoint of absolute safety, but also to create and maintain a feeling of security in the minds of all residents. Indeed, an independent engineer declared it one of the strongest dams in the world at the time. The brochure went on to state that this greater sense of security would also arise from the increased reserves of needed water, and by the reassuring thought that "seventy-five percent of the water in the Bow and Elbow Rivers comes from snow melt."

Calgary and Edmonton have experienced similar water problems over the course of their development, but have not always found similar solutions. Edmonton sought to relieve the pressure upon filtered and treated water by encouraging residents to dig their own wells for water to be used on gardens, lawns, backyard pools and car washing. Calgary's City Health Officer opposed private wells, arguing that some of the water from backyard wells was sure to be used for household purposes, and that there was a chance that it would be the means of spreading diseases like typhoid fever.

The groundwater policy in Edmonton has been quite popular and many property owners have said they have saved money by drawing on groundwater in addition to municipal supplies. The question many were concerned with was the acceptability of groundwater as an alternative to the more costly treated water from the municipal waterworks. "The Ground Water Option," a 1993 document published by the city, makes it clear that it is an excellent alternative in certain situations:

> *If your company uses water for industrial purposes such as cement production, washing, rinsing, cooling or other purposes where potable water is not needed, you are paying for more water quality than you need. Does your company need drinking quality water for process use? Beneath many parts of Edmonton are groundwater reservoirs which may be economically tapped by your firm at a cost lower than city potable water.*

After fifty years of often sarcastic inter-city debate about the net worth of water meters, Edmonton's charges for water were still meter based, and citizens were generally satisfied that their policy offered the best opportunities for conservation at less cost than would be possible with Calgary's flat rate plan. In the slow race for the most economical use of water, Edmonton was emerging as the clear winner. The single year of 1948 was a widely-used and telling example. During that year, Edmonton drew upon its waterworks for a total of fourteen billion litres, and Calgary, with its slightly smaller population, used twenty-eight billion litres.

This discrepancy in water use between the two cities was often invoked to embarrass the bigger and more profligate user. Levity was difficult to suppress, especially in Edmonton in the 1940s. One observer, after hearing of Calgary's record use of water, remarked, "Well, at last Calgary has surpassed Edmonton in a performance, but there is no trophy for the most extravagant use of water." Another, similarly unkind, said that Calgary's water system had too many holes in it, "just like the argument in favour of a flat rate for all municipal water customers."

For citizens of Calgary, the water metering debate developed such a personal character that many taxpayers said they were tired of hearing about it. Even the argument that the "Foothills City" could save millions in public money if it switched to metering was insufficient to produce a well supported programme of positive action.

People can be expected to resent compulsion, and dislike it even more when they know they must pay for it. After being reminded many times of Nature's benevolence in the form of mountain streams coming together as if designed to serve their great city, many Calgarians said, "If it was given to us to enjoy with freedom, let's hang on to it, and to the wasteful privileges too."

Of course, no public works are really free of costs: reservoirs, dams, towers, underground waterlines, to say nothing of furnishing filtering and treatment facilities and creating safeguards against pollution and human hazards, are expensive services. Taxpayers know they must accept these costs. Edmonton citizens, in general, have been the more compliant stewards of the water, and the more readily convinced that certain conservation measures were immediately worthy of their price. On the other hand, Calgarians were lured by the freedom of use or abuse of water privileges, applying it lavishly and wastefully on lawns and gardens, for instance, by allowing sprinklers to run all night regardless of need. Residents of the southern city continued to display a "stubborn streak" in the plebiscites of 1959 and 1966, rejecting universal metering as a means of curbing water waste on both occasions.

But metering proved that it can readily become an emotional subject, and it is highly probable that the principle of paying for the value received in water will inspire a few aldermen to continue their fight for universal metering of water. When and if they succeed, Calgary, the last important Canadian city to hold out against meters, will begin a wiser use of its wealth of sparkling mountain water.

Students of water problems are continually reminded that the generation of thermal power and manufacturing have been

Canada's largest users of water in recent years, but municipal uses do not follow that far behind. Urban dwellers like those in Edmonton and Calgary will find the greatest interest and concern in the widely-varied water duties falling to their urban administrators, and the pressing problems with municipal drinking water, supplies for parks, rinks, fire fighting, pollution control, street cleaning, flood control, water treatment and distribution, and much more. Municipal water usage offers varied opportunities for study.

To be a worthy custodian of the great gift of water, the servant of a municipality should be one who is ever ready to acknowledge a moral responsibility for the protection of the natural treasures far beyond the bounds of the district, regardless of who claims ownership. Calgary's and Edmonton's public servants should, indeed, evince equal concern over each other's water-use programmes.

Chapter Sixteen: Barbara Ward's Water Message

If we are greedy about this delicate planet, we shall simply have no planet. We can all cheat on morals. We all know that and I suspect we all do it. We rise above exhortations. We can forget moral imperatives. But today the morals of respect and care and modesty come to us in a form that we cannot evade. We cannot cheat on DNA. We cannot get around photosynthesis. We cannot say I am not going to give a damn about phytoplankton. All these tiny mechanisms provide the preconditions of our planetary life. To say that we do not care is to say in the most literal sense that "we choose death".

—Barbara Ward, 1973

In their rush to exploit their wealth of natural resources, North Americans have been rebuked from time to time for the greedy haste of their development, and the waste and extravagance that has accompanied it. They have found it difficult to accept the notion that resources such as oil, forests, soil and minerals belong to

A natural treasure: The falls on the Bow River, Banff, Alberta.
(Provincial Archives of Alberta, B 9597)

everyone. The business tycoons who see those resources as an opportunity to amass private wealth do not wish to think of these natural treasures as legacies to which all generations have a claim.

It took a 1976 lecture in Calgary by Barbara Ward, a distinguished English economist, journalist and environmental educator, to put before the plutocrats a reasoned environmental argument to which they could make no rebuttal. Many of those who heard her called her warnings an "environmental wake-up call" for Canadians.

When she met with the media before her talk, Ward told them that what she would be speaking about would probably be unpopular, as most current environmental news was bad news. She explained that her lecture would draw on her two recent books on the relationships between the human and natural environment, *Only the Earth* and *The Home of Man*. The former book, co-authored with René Dubos, was commissioned by the United Nations Conference on the Human Environment in 1972, and emerged from research by scientific and intellectual leaders from fifty-eight countries. Ward wrote *The Home of Man for Habitat*, the United Nations Conference on Human Settlements held in Vancouver in 1976. Growing out of this recent work, Ward's talk in Calgary proved to be one of the environmental highlights of the 1970s.

Ward made it quite clear that she was not in Alberta simply to tell influential Calgarians flattering things about themselves. Indeed, those people were soon to hear some challenging views that were less than complementary concerning their wealth and comfortable way of life. Without the slightest hint of bitterness or anger, she said that in her opinion, any province that can "stash away" billions of dollars in a "Heritage Trust Fund" should be doing more to advance its humanitarianism. Alberta should be sharing some of that wealth with less fortunate provinces, such as the Maritime provinces, and Canada should be taking similar steps to ensure that needy nations had enough food and clean water.

Canada, Ward opined, must pay very special attention to the rising urgency of resource conservation and environmental protection. Canadians should renounce their resource-depleting habits and become candidates for world leadership in conservation. In her mind, our country already possessed all the qualifications for this role because of its wealth in natural resources and its international reputation for diplomacy and peaceful, honest dealing. Ward advised,

> *If Canadians favour the idea of working as a coalition, let's work together with other countries like Norway, Sweden and Holland. None of them are excessively big or powerful or rich, but they are acknowledged humanitarians likely to inspire confidence in their leadership. Let's consider calling upon some of the broad-minded leaders of the Middle East who are prepared to contribute ten to twenty percent of their oil incomes.*

The Calgary gathering was told in sombre terms that whatever the composition of the environmental leadership, all reasonable haste should be taken to put into effect the ideals of conservation, economy and pollution control. If not, much more of our precious, non-renewable resources would be lost to waste and extravagance.

Ward's message was a further incentive for Canadians to act quickly and put their own environmental house in order. That, as everybody knew, was a big assignment, spread as it was over one of the biggest countries on the planet. And certainly, as a role model for conservation, the United States was not much help. "Wastefulness," Ward said, "is a way of life in North America." It was a sad but justifiable indictment. Ward added that if the wealthy nations of the world continued to burn and waste fossil fuels with such abandon, there would not be any left in two hundred years.

She brought home to Calgarians what she meant by "throwing energy around recklessly," referring to the big and heavy cars she saw on the streets of Calgary. Most of them had a single occupant who probably could have used some healthy exercise. Ward also referred to the widespread use of glass in the city's fashionable new buildings as "one of the poorest insulators on the market."

Throughout her talk, Ward drew upon her extensive work and travel in Africa, Asia and Central America, paying particular attention to those parts of the world where poverty, overpopulation, and inadequate water came together. Her principal complaints about the flaws in conservation and environmental protection, most of which grew out of an insufficient supply of fresh water, were global in scope. She believed that the impatience of hungry and thirsty people in developing countries was growing, and that they would not sit by much longer and watch the rich nations plunder the world's natural resources.

With the steady net growth in human population and the current shrinkage in the world's yield of food grains, Ward warned that a food grain deficit seemed inevitable. "We are getting ever closer to the limit of our ability to feed the members of our race," said Ward. "More than two billion children are malnourished today and eighty million more can be expected to arrive every year."

It was not a cheerful outlook, but Barbara Ward, more than most environmental prognosticators, stressed practical applications, including the identification of hitherto hidden reservoirs of groundwater, large-scale diversion projects, and more thoroughgoing research into economically viable desalination processes.

Nobody said it would be easy. Barbara Ward had seen the situation and its dangers at close range and knew the task would be both massive and messy, and no less serious than the shrinking corn and rice harvests around the world. Half of the world's population, she elaborated, did not have adequate supplies of water that were safe to drink, and polluted water was becoming a leading cause of death.

She had seen the centuries-old open sewers on the streets of Calcutta, demonstrating pollution at its worst. She had seen some of the most shocking results of water deprivation in Latin America where, according to the most reliable information, only about one-third of municipalities had either sewage or piped water systems. And what she could relate from Latin

America was no more disturbing than what had become obvious in many parts of Africa.

In her stand against swelling military budgets, Ward made two of her convictions very clear. First, she disapproved of the huge investments in weapons of war—estimated to be more than $300 billion a year—being made by developed nations. And secondly, she bluntly proposed that she would gladly undertake to use the entire total of military budgets to alleviate global inequities stemming from food and water shortages.

The current levels of military expenditure were an appalling waste since the total, if accumulated over the next ten years, would be sufficient to pay the cost of making pure water available to every settlement in the world. "Such a service," she said, "would do more than any other single benefit for the world's people; and any society that can spend $300 billion on defence can spend at least three billion on water."

Ward's dream of a huge investment in the provision of water whenever and wherever there was human need has never been realized. She knew the immense cost of moving water would present problems, but she was reluctant to accept it as an obstacle. It is doubtful whether anybody could have made a better effort to make the worthy project succeed. The enormous task she proposed still beckons. Her appeals for funds were not ignored, but the response was not overwhelming. Clean water was not an easy thing to build a development campaign around. Ward had supporters, though, who gave handsomely, and there were stories of the generosity of little people such as the twelve-year-old Alberta farm girl who emptied her piggy bank and sent her savings away to Barbara

Ward's Water Fund. Her donation of one dollar and eighty cents was later acknowledged in a letter informing the girl that her money had been invested in a shovel for use in digging a family well in West Africa.

Good water is always a blessing, and those who are privileged enough to have it should not imagine that everyone is so fortunate.

Chapter Seventeen: The Threat of Pollution

Ye who would raise a hand to me, hearken ere you harm me. I am the best of your hearth on cold winter nights, the friendly shade screening you from the summer sun and my fruits are refreshing draughts quenching your thirst as you journey on. I am the beam that holds your house, the board of your table, the bed on which you lie, the timber that builds your boat. I am the handle of your hoe, the door of your homestead, the wood of your cradle and the shell of your coffin. I am the gift of god and the friend of man.

—From a sign found hanging on an English park tree in 1960

Judging from the long history of pollution, it would be easy to suppose that water has an affinity for evil companions, or that pollutants have an affinity for water. Whatever the case may be, pollution takes innumerable forms, sometimes visible, sometimes invisible, and often difficult to trace to a place of origin. It is but a happy

The Swan Hills, Alberta oil spill clean up Operation, 1975.
(Provincial Archives of Alberta, J 1892)

dream at present that any or all of the world's offending pollutants can be traced and destroyed before becoming menacing on a large scale. The most offensive pollutants can very readily escape the naked eye and some, such as mercury and dioxin, can be deadly. High levels of mercury in American lakes have meant that fish caught in thousands of them are unfit for human consumption. Dioxin, a carcinogenic by-product from the manufacture of agricultural chemicals, has similarly frightening potential.

Left unaddressed, new and powerful pollution dangers could readily emerge from ongoing human activity. There is risk in every flood or run-off that dangerous materials will wash into the water system from communities, sewage plants, winter accumulations of barnyard manure, or the seepage of pesticides and fertilizers from farm fields where application was too lavish. Given favourable conditions, the nitrogenous compounds that make up agricultural fertilizers can become a danger to the ecosystem. This means that farmers and other users of new chemicals must possess a firm grasp of chemistry or be in a position to place their utmost confidence in highly qualified public servants.

Lake Victoria, the biggest fresh water lake in Africa and the second biggest in the world (after Lake Superior) is in peril. It hovers perilously close to being classified as a "dead lake," one which can no longer support life. The rapid increase in population density and the changing character of local industry have been regarded as important forces in the deterioration of the lake but not the only ones. Once a natural showpiece, Lake Victoria followed an increasingly familiar course. It became overly popular with travellers and residents and soon suffered from the indiscriminate dumping of sewage and the accumulation of fertilizers. This led to an excessive build-up of water weeds and algae, which in turn deprived the lake's fish and other life forms of oxygen.

On a smaller scale, this chain of events is being played out on many lakes, including the second smallest of the Great Lakes, Lake Erie. Even the explorers and first settlers saw Erie and its surroundings as an especially attractive region, rich in birds, forests and fish. There were scenic wonders such as the Niagara Falls and, later, man-made ones like the Welland Canal. Predictably, the overwhelming appeal of the lake led to pollution that saw it become almost uninhabitable for fish. For a long time, admirers of the lake despaired of ever seeing the recovery of this once lovely body of water. Recent efforts at rejuvenation, however, will hopefully prove them wrong.

With the growing public concern about pollution and contamination dangers to public water supplies, the establishment of the Pollution Probe Foundation in 1969 came like a proverbial blessing in disguise. Many influential Canadian and American citizens voiced their support of the Foundation. Investigation and research were, as its name suggested, the original purposes of the Foundation. It would be easy to presume that the dioxin scare had much to do with its inception. Spokesmen for the Foundation admitted an official interest in all aspects of environmentalism, making the organization a virtual pioneer in that branch of study. Also winning special attention was the study of acid rain, which was composed of two particular acids, sulphur oxide and nitrogen oxide.

Carried from exhaust pipes or smoke stacks high into the atmosphere, these acids attach themselves to rain or snow and return to earth as full-fledged pollutants.

Discussion of acid rain became commonplace on Canadian and American streets during the 1960s. Farmers, editors and school teachers took to consulting the handy acid-alkaline tables which indicate the pH value of various substances. A pH figure is taken to indicate the degree of concentration of hydrogen ions in a sample's chemical components. The point of neutrality between acid and alkali on the pH scale was given the value of 7. At the low end, something as acidic as vinegar has a pH of 2.2. For seawater, the pH is about 8.5, and rainwater, after acquiring a slight amount of acidification from carbon dioxide, is likely to earn a value of 5.6. Most kinds of fish will have difficulty surviving in water with a pH level below 4.

Much of the reason for the total absence of fish in hundreds of eastern North American lakes lies in their increased acidification in recent years. Indeed, it is probable that some of the afflicted species may not survive. What, then, is to be done to protect water, soil and vegetation from the pollutants derived from fossil fuel exhaust and harmful emissions from industrial plants? Better control of these emissions must surely be on the way. Higher smoke stacks have been tried as a solution, but it was found that although they eased the pollution in the immediate area of the plants, the offending fumes were simply broadcast more widely. Where there is some choice, low-sulphur fuels, which burn cleaner than the high-sulphur varieties, have been found to lessen the acid rain-producing discharges.

Throughout the 1970s, Eastern Canadians blamed the

heavily industrialized cities across the United States border for the acid rain pollution delivered by the winds. But in the West, the reverse was occasionally seen to be the case. American farmers down-wind from the big Consolidated Mining and Smelting Company at Trail, British Columbia had long wondered why they were having difficulty with their crops. They concluded that something in the fumes from the big smelter was responsible. They were correct in their assessment but were uninformed about the exact nature of the chemical imbalance. Shortly thereafter, the Wenatchee Valley Fruit Growers, also south of Trail, brought the Consolidated Mining and Smelting Company to court and were successful in forcing it to institute more rigorous emission controls.

All the governments in the heavily populated parts of the world, it seemed, were failing to take into account the threat of acid rain. A prime example was the Great Lakes region, long the joint pride of both Canadians and Americans, where water quality had been declining over a long period of time. In 1972, Lake Erie was found to have a high concentration of DAT in its water. As late as 1994, newspapers were reporting that pollution in the Great Lakes was at record high levels. Representatives from the United States and Canada have met from time to time to make and sign agreements for ending pollution and restoring former water quality to the Great Lakes, but the results have never measured up to hopes and expectations. A report out of Ottawa in late 1995 confirmed that four years after the triumphant signing of the Canada-United States acid rain treaty, the great environmental issue of the 1970s and 80s was due for an unwelcome comeback.

Elsewhere in Canada, Dennis McDonald of the Canadian Fish and Wildlife Service told a western audience that just as the best varieties of fish had died out in Lake Erie, so many of the best kinds of fish in the Bow River below Calgary "may soon be gone forever." McDonald was angered by those who scoffed at the concern being shown about a few dead fish. "The all-important message," he declared with clan McDonald forcefulness, "is if man succeeds in wiping out the life cycle of lower, more sensitive forms of life, then it is only a matter of time before he follows the same pattern."

Even small-scale pollution can have serious effects. This author will not soon forget the experience of a Saskatchewan farmer who unwisely created a small oil spill in a slough and was not allowed to forget it. It looked like neither a big nor serious danger to water birds at first, but as a sensitive bird-lover, this author became their self-appointed monitor, reporting each day upon the number of new deaths of mallard ducks with oil-soaked feathers. So emotionally dismayed was their monitor that he issued a challenge to local bird lovers that they undertake to pump the lake dry and dump the polluted sludge down an abandoned oil well. No action was taken, however, and the feathered skeletons were still visible a year later.

On the oceanic front, one of the most devastating sources of world-wide pollution is the typical petroleum tanker, the work-horse of the oil industry, capable of carrying up to a hundred million litres of oil. When these enormous vessels experience trouble, be it an oil leak or a full-fledged spill, it is sure to be "big trouble." Spills from ships in the 1950s and 60s were quite limited, though in most cases extensive clean-up procedures were not followed. Recently, the big ocean spills, which seem to be occurring with increasing frequency, have happened in both remote areas where prompt help is impossible, and along more populated coastlines where the ghastly damage wrought by the oil is most apparent. "Ugly" and "devastating" are the only terms appropriate for the repulsive aftermath.

Oil spills from tankers occur not only when they run aground, but are sometimes deliberately made in the course of a tanker's clean-up operations. These small discharges are just a big spill on a small scale. These practices persist largely because of the ease with which they escape public notice. Deliberate spillage continues to be a lazy and unscrupulous way of dealing with waste associated with the cleaning of these ships.

The loss of a cargo of oil is commonly only a small part of the total cost of a spill. Not to be overlooked is the damage done to waterfront parks and resort areas. The most shocking of all, however, is the inestimable suffering and death brought to undetermined numbers of marine life, including fish, water birds and marine mammals. Years after the highly publicized Exxon Valdez spill in Alaskan waters, there was still doubt as to whether some of the species of seals that had suffered the heaviest losses would ever recover their former numbers.

The recent push to reinforce oil tankers' hulls with additional layers of metal has been a step in the right direction. There is still no guarantee, though, that all the risks and dangers confronting a loaded tanker on the long routes between the gigantic oil fields of the Far and Middle East and their distant markets will be entirely eliminated. The Americans, as might be expected, were the first to declare faith in the benefits of double hulls for oil tankers. After the Exxon Valdez accident, the United States Congress was quick to pass legislation which addressed this issue. The Oil Pollution Act of 1990 made it mandatory for all new oil tankers ordered for construction after June 1990 to be equipped with double hulls. Furthermore, all tankers with single hulls were to be phased out by the year 2015. A Washington leader stated with self-assurance that "if the double hulls do not reduce our troubles on the sea-lanes, we will demand the adoption of three-ply metal."

The subsequent phasing in of double-hulled tankers has probably done something to reduce losses at sea, but accidents and disasters have continued to plague the big carriers. Human error and the sheer "cussedness" of the weather can never be entirely overcome.

Nor has the joint programme conducted by the two North American neighbours been consistently successful in the battle against pollution in the Great Lakes. Joint political conferences have resulted in optimistic promises and more than a billion dollars in expenditures. But the optimism generated at one conference has not always lasted until the next one. It has not been easy to determine whether the net results of these recent years of anti-pollution campaigning have been clearly positive or negative. It has too often depended upon which politicians were the last to be consulted. That, of course, could change. In 1994, the Canadian Environment Minister, Sheila Copps, promised to spend a quarter of a billion dollars to clean up the

Great Lakes and the St. Lawrence River by the year 2000. She set out the programme with all apparent conviction. Her personal pledge, by which she chose to be remembered, was that "Great Lakes 2000 will yield drinkable, fishable, swimmable water, and return national waters to the people on shore." Even sceptics such as the editors of the *Globe and Mail* have conceded that this most recent promise has the best chance of success.

Chapter Eighteen: Selling Canada's Water

The word, "conservation," with its present con-notation, was unknown until the early part of 1907. It occurred to me one day that forestry, irrigation, soil protection, flood control, water power and a lot of other matters were up to that time kept in separate watertight compartments, all parts of one problem. The problem was and is the use of the whole earth and all of the resources for the enduring good of mankind.

—Gifford Pinchet, 1955

Water shortages, as causes of suffering and premature death, should stand along-side the more highly publicized food famines in terms of catastrophic magnitude. The highly regarded *Christian Science Monitor* recently informed its readers that "almost one out of every three people in the developing parts of Africa and Asia, does not have access to safe and reliable supplies of drinking water for family needs." More fortunate citizens in other parts of the world will say they have heard all of that before, but they should not and dare not close their

*A creek near Whitecourt, Alberta: a small part of
Canada's renewable fresh water supply.*
(D. Shawn Kabatoff / Vision Images)

eyes to a sorrowful dilemma that makes world water problems a serious threat to humanity in every region of the world.

North Americans following the daily news could easily be misled into thinking that resources like oil, natural gas, silver and gold are today's most precious treasures. As important as these may be, they must not be rated above water, soil, trees, and air. These foundations of life should be cherished and deserve to be safeguarded diligently against waste and greedy exploitation.

It is not difficult to hold the attention of an audience with talk of conservation when local water supplies are in decline. What is to be said for a situation in which one party has a far larger number of people and consequently the greater need for new sources of water, while another party has water resources in abundance but an unwillingness to trade?

The story of Canadian and American negotiations over water is a long one that began with the 1783 Treaty of Paris after the War of Independence. The international boundary between New Brunswick and Maine was to begin at the mouth of the St. Croix River. Among the many points of dispute that arose was the fact that there were three St. Croix Rivers on that side of the continent. It took the Ashburton-Webster Boundary Commission of 1842 to determine which one was intended to become the boundary marker.

Canadians have shown interest at various times in export sales of their water, anticipating the large sums of money that would come with such a sale. But they haven't forgotten the occasion when the Americans were too sharp for their neighbours and left a hideously crooked international border between New Brunswick and the State of Maine as an unforgettable reminder. That was not the only geographical remnant of extremely hard bargaining on the part of the United States. There was the equally memorable Alaskan boundary dispute that dragged on and on and ultimately deprived Canadians of a vast stretch of Pacific coastline—what came to be infamously known as the "Alaska Panhandle."

It wasn't surprising then that when the two ageing neighbours began negotiating a massive Free Trade deal in the late 1980s, the Canadian negotiators braced themselves to protect the wealth of water scattered across the north of the country. "It has become very largely a mix of pride and sentiment and prejudice," said one of the Canadian negotiators, "and both sides will be at their stubborn best when water is 'on the table,' you can be sure."

One of the stubborn spirits who followed the Free Trade negotiations with patience complained of the deep rift that ran through the ranks of the conservationists. Many of them were ready to deal away our non-renewable oil and natural gas resources with what sometimes seemed like "indecent haste." At the same time, the majority stood with relative firmness against the principle of selling fresh water for export, even though it is the most easily renewable of all resources.

The issue boils down to this: Canada has a relatively small population and vast unused quantities of high-grade water while the United States, with its much larger population, is desperately in need of it. A substantial number of Canadians are quietly opposed to an export sale; some even admit that they would prefer to see their good Canadian water lost in the salty brine of the Arctic. People are entitled to their opinions, but no effort should be spared in preventing important water decisions from falling to those in public life who are clearly motivated by personal and political gains.

The fact that nine percent of the world's renewable fresh water is in Canada's backyard should elicit enthusiastic gratitude from Canadians everywhere and generate a charitable feeling for water-needy people wherever they may be. Western Canada, even though it is well-acquainted with drought, can still fill its international neighbours with envy. The people of Alberta, after giving thanks for the rich gifts of oil, natural gas, soil and coal, should not forget their incredible legacy of water, even though its distribution around the province has been less than ideal. Most of the irrigation in Canada is in Alberta. Although it is not considered an extensive industry, it is important. It seems likely that greater agricultural productivity will develop as water that flows through southern Alberta today is further diverted to irrigation.

If irrigation or other uses are not found for Canada's surplus water, the case for export sale will be greatly strengthened. There is nothing to be said for letting the Mackenzie and Nelson water drain fruitlessly into the Arctic Ocean. Yet recent opinion polls show that about fifty-seven percent of respondents are in favour of strictly controlled water sales, and that only seven percent support export sales without predetermined controls.

A wider distribution of Canadian water could help ease the suffering due to water scarcity felt by young and old, needy and poverty-stricken, humans and animals in an increasing number of countries. It will not become any easier to negotiate with them in the future. The ones with urgent needs will become more and more adamant. Canadians have seen in the past that when water becomes attractive for export it acquires instant political sensitivity.

Canadians can expect to participate in important plebiscites on water in the years ahead. Even without possessing the qualifications of trained hydro-engineers, ordinary citizens should accept their responsibilities with diligence and review the growing history of water fortunes and misfortunes in our nation. The water in any future trade deal belongs to the voters and their children, and deserves the most thorough possible consideration.

Anyone who is searching for biblical instruction in the matter of exporting fresh water from the Canadian North should look to the writings of St. Paul to the Romans: "If thine enemy hungers, feed him; if he thirsts, give him drink..." (Romans 12:20). It is safe to say that St. Paul was not thinking about water exports; what he was thinking about, undoubtedly, was old-fashioned charity, which should never go out of date. Charity should be enshrined in human memory along with the unfading lustre of water itself, a natural phenomenon that never rests, never gives up, never wears out, never surrenders to the forces of destruction and never fails to bring restoration to God's beautiful and much buffeted world.

What answers does tomorrow's technology and inventiveness hold for the world's domestic water needs? One of the first and largest desalination plants in the world was in Kuwait, funded by the country's prodigious oil revenues.

Kuwait was also one of the few markets in which a barrel of
fresh water might have commanded the same price as a barrel
of oil. Canadians and others will hear more about desalination
practices when energy costs are further reduced. Then the
long-awaited hope of making salty or brackish water acceptable for use in homes, factories and irrigation will become
standard practice.

Students of these new practices in water use should not
be allowed to forget that they are still a part of the all-encom-
passing water cycle. Human beings, quite fairly, have seen it
as their privilege to capture portions of that underground
water, generally through wells, as it continues on its way.
Recently, experts have determined that North American
groundwater exceeds in volume all the surface water in lakes,
ponds and rivers. These estimates cast new light on the wealth
of the continent's abundant water resources, while raising
new fears about damaging the intricate environmental system
which took millenia to develop.

Still, what could conceivably become the most compelling
new achievement in water invention? It could well prove to be
a long-awaited scientific breakthrough that would give tidal
power the better economic face it needs. If and when it happens, Canadians can expect Nova Scotia's fortunes to surge
like a Fundy tide. North Americans living near the Bay of
Fundy witness the biggest inflow and outflow of tidal water in
the world. They should be reminded of what this can mean in
potential hydro power.

Ocean tides, it seems, never rest; they reflect the periodic
rise and fall of the incoming flood tide and outgoing ebb tide

as they respond to the gravitational influences of the moon and sun. Herein lies one of the unique features of tidal power: the same water is capable of generating power when it is both coming and going on successive tides, and the height of tides rarely vary by much. Unfailingly regular, they act as if they were serving the role of the earth's official timekeeper, with their two high tides and two low tides in each lunar day of twenty-four hours and fifty-one minutes.

The potential energy that tides represent has long been recognized. In fact, the powerful tides of Maritime Canada's Bay of Fundy were the first form of hydro power to be harnessed in the western hemisphere. At Port Royal in 1607, the French installed a water wheel and mill supervised by Baron de Poutrincourt, fellow worker with Samuel de Champlain. The tidal water powered the grist mill there for several years, presumably with satisfactory results. Tidewater may appear boisterous at times but it is never still and should be used more effectively.

As the end of this book on water draws near, this author is reminded that this project began on a theme of conservation and is now being inexorably pulled, as if by magnetic attraction, toward that same, solemn theme. When this final chapter was underway, one of the most striking headlines in the world's press reported the death of what scientists called the last member of a now-extinct species, the Polynesian tree snail. It didn't seem to matter much that the lowly animal was one that most people had never seen, nor, indeed, heard of before. What mattered was that here was a species which, according to scientists, had been a global resident for one-and-a-half million years before giving up the struggle and entering the long black night of extinction.

Every living race has had its distinctions to set it apart and the tree snail was certainly no exception. It seems unfortunate that most humans would be content to wait until the species had disappeared before taking note of the animal world's champion of slow motion, whose average rate of locomotion was just sixty centimetres a year.

The tree snail's rate of travel was, of course, its own business. But it should not go unnoticed that, of the many thousands of living species that have disappeared forever, only a few cases have been historically documented. Where this information does exist, it furnishes the best lessons in wildlife conservation, as in the instances of the passenger pigeon and great auk. These are stories that should be told and retold at every possible opportunity, especially to the young.

It was on September 1, 1914, that the twenty-nine-year-old passenger pigeon known as Martha died in the Cincinnati Zoo and took her race with her. A race that once numbered billions of birds, the passenger pigeon may once have been the most conspicuous bird in the North American skies. It is a sad story but one that should be accorded special recognition on Conservation Day, held annually on the first day of September.

Utterly unlike the passenger pigeon, the great auk was a large, penguin-like bird capable of staying for long spells under water. Like the passenger pigeon, one of its misfortunes was that its flesh was extremely attractive to human consumers. This ultimately led to its sudden demise. The death of the last remaining birds came, it seems, by means of clubs in the hands of hunters who went to Eldey Rock on Funk Island in the North Atlantic to collect a supply of auk meat. On June 3, 1844, finding only one pair of the game fowl on the island, the hunters clubbed and bagged the two birds. Taking the two birds was an easy exercise, but tragic in its finality. Canadians and other visitors to the islands have no hope of ever seeing the beautiful and fascinating "Atlantic penguins" again.

It is something that is happening every day beyond our notice. It shouldn't be beyond our care. What the extinction of the Polynesian tree snail should remind us of is the interconnection of all living things. The disappearance of another species from the earth affects the quality of human life, regardless of whether we immediately recognize it. In our drive to develop, we have altered the nature of the intricate interrelationships between ourselves and our environment. The world's precious reserves of fossil fuels, fish, air, forests, wildlife, soil, water and much more are showing signs of either depletion or deterioration. Water itself is the most "renewable" of resources and is wonderfully resilient. The increasing use of water, in step with the accelerating pace of human activity, is putting extraordinary pressure on the mighty water wheel's ability to cleanse itself. Our ability to pollute water outstrips its ability to purify itself by a wide margin. We must find a new balance between our expectations, our seemingly limitless appetites, and the supplies of water that ensure our survival. Miraculous though it often strikes us, water cannot flush away the problems of our own making.

Change begins with a sense of stewardship which itself grows out of understanding. The more we seek to know our environment and the history of our relationship with it, the more we will see a much clearer course for change. The concern that grows out of understanding should fuel our desire for concerted action. The time has come for us to make hard and judicious choices that will have a great effect on those who come after us. The care and responsibility we show for our water demonstrates much about our values, including our level of concern for the quality of life of future generations.

Grant MacEwan on his raft on the South Saskatchewan River in 1931.
(MacEwan Family Archives)

PART VII: WATER PLEASURE: A RAFT ON THE SOUTH SASKATCHEWAN

Some time ago I had the opportunity to talk to a former homesteader who had filed on a plot of land in the grasslands of southwestern Saskatchewan. In this arid region legend had it that frogs died without ever having learned to swim. A man of cheerful disposition, the homesteader still held on to many happy memories of water recreation during the time he spent in the region. The foremost of these was that of his annual spring shower baths, which he said consisted of "one or two sprinkling cans of warm, soft water hung on a harness hook in the horse stable."

If he liked it that much, I asked, why didn't he repeat it more often? "Because," he explained, "there wasn't any more soft water to spare." He may have been exaggerating, but probably not. Like many of his generation, he learned to swim in a Canadian Pacific Railway ditch. Some learned very well, especially those who came under the coaching influence of instructors like Joe Griffiths, trainer extraordinaire and Prince of Gentlemen who was for many years the director of physical education at the University of Saskatchewan. "Making swimmers out of prairie kids," he said, "was my lifetime goal."

Prairie young people of the frontier years were, for one reason or another, likely to terminate plans for high school studies. The distances between farm houses and high school facilities were, of course, a principal reason. But this was a temporary situation and many of the drop-outs heard the call to return to schools after they began offering gymnasiums, playing fields and even access to indoor swimming facilities. As the years advanced, new schools were built with their own pools. But if Joe Griffiths had been a spectator of this change, he probably would have repeated his conviction: some of the best swimmers Canada had ever sent to international competitions were kids who had learned to dog-paddle in a railroad ditch in the Palliser Triangle.

Even in the 1930s, when drought and economic depression were tightening their cruel grip on much of the world, when the prairies became a dust bowl and wheat prices collapsed, when university employees who usually took summer holidays gave them up, water recreation was still available for little or no cost. One late August evening in 1931, Alister Ewen, my new colleague at the University of Saskatchewan, and I had an idea for an inexpensive holiday. It occurred to us as we were walking to our living quarters across the broad South Saskatchewan River. Why not take a rafting trip down the South Saskatchewan River just like in the days of the fur trade? Henry David Thoreau, who said "the man is the richest whose pleasures are the cheapest," would have nodded his approval of the plan. Al Ewen quickly warmed to the idea even though he didn't know exactly what to expect from the proposed log raft expedition. A graduate of the University of Edinburgh, he was a versatile athlete, a strong swimmer and a former heavyweight boxing champion of the Scottish universities. He knew nothing about the Saskatchewan River but would be an excellent partner on the journey.

Plans were completed in the half hour it took to walk home that summer evening, and everything fell into place like a well-oiled army manoeuvre. I happened to know somebody in the service of the Saskatchewan Telephone Company and was sure I could buy three or four discarded telephone poles at a bargain price and have them delivered early on the same day. After these sixty-centimetre-thick poles were delivered to a Saskatoon river bank and cut in half, the budding raft mariners had eight raft poles three-and-a-half metres in length. Our material investment had been nominal: a dollar each for the four ageing poles with an additional dollar spent on rope for lashing them together. The assembled raft weighed close to three-quarters of a tonne. Thankfully, the raft, cumbersome on shore, became agreeably submissive once it was eased into the water. We would later come to understand how we had over-estimated the stability of our raft and underestimated the power of the river.

Mounted with a packing-box shelter, the raft was pushed into midstream at 3:30 PM on launching day, leaving behind on the shore some twenty envious kids and one snarky fellow who wanted to know how the merry adventurers were going to find their way back to the city.

The first full night on the river had an almost divine peacefulness about it. The only person in sight when the travellers awakened was a farmer who had driven his horses to the river to drink. Eager to know how far the raft had travelled during the night, Al asked him how far it was to Saskatoon. "Heck man, you've passed Saskatoon," the farmer replied. "You'll never get there now."

The second night on the water was more alarming. First there came a storm that seemed to be trying to blow the travellers back to Saskatoon. Following a lull, another storm hit, this time accompanied by lightning. The drenched travellers found some solace in the knowledge that the safest place to be in a lightning storm might well be on a raft in the middle of a river.

For the intrepid rafters of August 1931, there were new experiences and water adventures at every bend in the river. A heavy raft riding peacefully on quiet water is not likely to make trouble. On the other hand, the same raft with a great weight of angry water behind it can easily perform an aerial flip.

Disaster struck near Fenton Ferry just minutes after we had bought our mid-journey groceries. The crowning glory was a four-pound can of peach jam that was supposed to furnish a special meal-time treat for the next few days. The treacherous water ahead seemed innocuous enough to two mariners who now thought themselves thoroughly seasoned. After all, the loaded raft represented almost a full tonne of weight and promised stability. MacEwan, with his seven-foot staff, was at the front and would be the first to sense danger and change navigational orders accordingly if necessary. It was the job of the man at the front to decide which side of an exposed rock appeared to be the safest for the raft.

A threatening rock was indeed sighted, but merely sighting it was to no avail. As the roar of water about the rock grew more deafening, it became obvious that it would be impossible for us to change course. All self-assurance about the stability of the heavy raft evaporated like a spray of hot water in the desert.

It isn't difficult to explain what happened. Locked in the rush of the current, the front of the raft struck the protruding rock like a battering ram, slid up one side of it and tilted, sending everything aboard cascading into the turbulent waters; blankets, clothing and the four-pound can of peach jam hit the water along with the hapless adventurers. Luckily, when we resurfaced we caught the two lower corners of the upended raft. We clung to it dangerously until we could find a way of shifting the raft slightly, creating a new imbalance sufficient to cause it to right itself and fall flat again. Through sheer determination, we succeeded in doing so and then retrieved as much of the inadvertent jetsam as possible. Sadly, the four-pound can of jam had sunk like a stone to become a treasure lodged forever beneath the current. To this day, this author can remember exactly where the accident took place and confidently predicts that, given favourable circumstances, he could still retrieve the jam and enjoy the meal he never had on that fateful day in 1931.

Over the course of six days we had drifted one hundred and sixty kilometres down the broad river. The entry in this author's diary following the grand adventure read: "It was a great holiday, simple, thrilling and cheap. The entire outing including the cost of the raft and equipment, food, return train fare, and a few incidentals, cost the travellers just twelve dollars each."

As for the historic South Saskatchewan, it remains as beautiful and capricious as ever. Al Ewen and I intended, at one time, to return to study the history of the forks area of the North and South Saskatchewan Rivers in greater detail. Sadly, fate and circumstance intervened and a second trip was never undertaken. Nevertheless, we were able to declare publicly that, in spite of a few errors and hazards, the 1931 log raft expedition on the South Saskatchewan River was the most memorable water holiday of our lives. If Henry David Thoreau had been present, he probably would have said with a smile, "What did I tell you?"

AFTERWORD

In 1993, as one of the founding members of the J.W. Grant MacEwan Environmental Studies Institute, I had the pleasure to introduce Dr. MacEwan as an inaugural speaker in a seminar series, hosted at the college that bears his name. Dr. MacEwan said he was going to talk about an idea he was developing for a book.

The audience in the filled-to-capacity lecture theatre that day was a typical Grant MacEwan crowd. It included many seniors, some with their grandchildren, many college faculty and students and some keen environmentalists who, like myself, expected the major thrust of Dr. MacEwan's talk to recommend the conservation of water, our most valuable resource.

In my introduction I talked of the respect that Albertans had for the environmental opinions of Dr. MacEwan, who had consistently promoted the wise use and conservation of our natural resources. I also alluded to some quotes from the bible that summarized two opposite opinions about water: that it is so plentiful that it can be used without thought and that it is more precious than gold. I asked the audience to consider which of these divergent views they expected that Dr. MacEwan would hold—knowing well what everyone, including myself, expected the answer to be. Then Dr. MacEwan spoke.

This rather fragile man with failing hearing came to centre stage and, with his booming voice, regaled the audience for over an hour with an insightful, and often humorous talk.

He started by discussing the hardships many western Canadian settlers, including his family, faced, with the threat of drought being the worst, then he went on to talk about water globally—specifically about how our blue planet, seemingly awash in water, is a fallacy. Only about two and a half percent of the water on earth is fresh, the rest is salty and unusable for drinking or irrigation. Of the fresh water, much is locked into glaciers or ice caps, so only a fraction of one percent of the earth's water is both drinkable and renewed by the water cycle each year.

This water, however, he said, is not distributed equally. We in Canada are lucky. From the myriad lakes of the shield to the huge inland "seas" of the Great Lakes to the mighty rivers, many take water for granted. However, this is not the case for the "dry land" farmers of southern Alberta and Saskatchewan.

The very viability of their farms and the communities that the farmers of Saskatchewan and Alberta support depends on the ability to dam and divert natural water systems like the Milk River to irrigate the land. The resulting disruption of natural wetland ecosystems, including loss of sustaining habitats for plants and animals, and the leaching and salinization of irrigated soils, are major concerns. Nothing is simple, said MacEwan.

Even among water-rich Canadians, there is friction. Imagine the controversy that would ensue if the governments of Alberta, British Columbia and the Northwest Territories decided, through a system of dams and river diversions, to channel water bound for the Arctic via the Mackenzie, through the Rocky Mountain trench to the water-starved parts of Canada. Imagine even more outrage if this water was destined to be sold to the southwestern United States.

After his introduction, I expected Dr. MacEwan to conclude his talk by championing the "environmental" view—that this plan could damage so much of our natural heritage and lead to unexpected ecological repercussions; therefore, a grand diversion scheme should never be implemented. I was wrong. Dr. MacEwan suggested that it was our duty to provide freshwater to those in need—not as a commodity to be sold but to be given away! On that day I learned something new about Grant MacEwan. He was an environmentalist—dead against the wasteful use of any natural resource and a strong proponent of conservation—but he was first and foremost a humanist Christian. His pioneer experiences, his studies, and living through the dust bowl days of the 1930's had reinforced the idea that if a neighbor is in need of anything, you share. Especially if it is that most valuable of all resources—water.

Sadly, Dr. MacEwan passed away in the early summer of 2000. As my seven year old daughter and I passed his simple coffin, lying in state at the Alberta legislature, I thought about many things: about how this man who had led a political party and represented the Queen in Alberta could also relate to pre-school children by telling them a story about squirrels; about a man who was respected by provincial premiers but could engage anyone in conversation and make them feel at ease; about a man who was an agriculturalist but cared so much about preserving life that he was a vegetarian. And I thought about a man who had clear priorities and who could always surprise.

Michael Stock, Ph.D.
Grant MacEwan College, Edmonton

Grant MacEwan as a young man in 1930
(MacEwan Family Archives)